# 52-WEEK FAMILY DEVOTIONAL

# ≈ 52-WEEK ≈
# FAMILY
# DEVOTIONAL

## A Year of Scripture, Activities, and Prayers to Grow Together with God

**By Luke MacDonald and Kristen MacDonald**

ROCKRIDGE
PRESS

First Rockridge Press trade paperback edition 2022

Rockridge Press and the Rockridge Press logo are trademarks or registered trademarks of Callisto Media Inc. and/or its affiliates in the United States and other countries and may not be used without written permission.

For general information on our other products and services, please contact our Customer Care Department within the United States at (866) 744-2665, or outside the United States at (510) 253-0500.

Hardcover ISBN: 979-8-88608-606-5 | Paperback ISBN: 978-1-68539-976-4
eBook ISBN: 978-1-63807-513-4

Manufactured in the United States of America

Interior and Cover Designer: Linda Snorina
Art Producer: Hannah Dickerson
Editor: Mo Mozuch
Production Editor: Nora Milman
Production Manager: Jose Olivera

All images used under license from Shutterstock.com

Author photo courtesy of Katy Carl Photography

10 9 8 7 6 5 4 3 2 1 0

To the **#housefullofmacboys**
and **#felicityrulestheroost**,
who encourage and challenge
our faith daily to be authentic.
We pray 3 John 1:4 for you.

# Contents

## Devotionals

# Introduction

**W**elcome to our kitchen table; pull up a chair. We have found our dining table to be one of the best places to discuss faith. Our family is rowdy and has a ton of energy, so over the years we've realized that if we talk about Jesus while we eat it goes a lot better than sitting in a circle singing "Kumbaya." This book is set up for a busy family. We have put together fifty-two weekly devotionals, each with a Bible verse, brief commentary, discussion questions, and family activities. We hope you will find it useful. We suggest taking the whole week to complete all the activities and actions, but only do one week at a time. Our hope is that you will unveil some things that your family really enjoys doing together and we pray they will draw you together as you discuss God's Word and how it applies to your lives.

We are Luke and Kristen MacDonald. We lead a church called Good News in the Neighborhood in the suburbs of Chicago. Together, we have been in ministry in a variety of ways since we were engaged to be married fifteen years ago. The most challenging ministry has been Kristen leading our brood of four through devotions since they were little. We believe what it says in Deuteronomy 6:4–7, that in order for our children—and ultimately our family—to love God with all our hearts and souls and strength and minds, it's not just about one check mark or verse that is read but a continual conversation throughout the days and weeks that is applicable to our lives—and it is love put into action. Through weekly dialogue and the ability to focus on a verse, discuss its meaning, apply it to your lives, and take action based on what it says, your family can bear fruit that wouldn't come otherwise.

In this devotional, we will use the NIV translation, but you can use any translation. Sometimes it's even helpful to look up multiple translations in order to gain understanding. No matter what your family's religious background or denomination, this book can help. Hebrews 4:12 says that "the word of God is alive and active" and "sharper than any double-edged sword," which means that when applied to your life it can change and mold and shape you like nothing else. Pull up an extra seat and pour (or spill!) a cup of coffee. You are welcomed here with open arms, and we will learn together as we study the best book we know. As our boys always say, *let'sssss goooo!*

# How to Use a Family Devotional

We want to encourage you to do this together. Set aside a time once per week, whether that is Saturday morning breakfast, before everyone heads to work and school, or maybe a night of the week you don't have extracurricular activities. Sit down and read the devotion for each of the fifty-two weeks together. We have found it best to have one person lead the devotion and then engage the entire family through discussion, reading through the verse, and applying the material. You may be surprised at how even your youngest children can recite or chime in with something they are learning. With the young ones, it's okay if every time does not go smoothly, or if they blurt out or struggle to connect. Sometimes encouraging them with a treat when they are done or even giving them a toy to play with as they listen helps them not disrupt the other members of the family. The rhythm of the weekly ritual will take time to bear fruit. Remember, everyone digests differently, so allow time and patience for all your different ages and temperaments.

We have prayerfully shared questions we would ask our own kids and activities and action steps that coincide with each verse. By no means do you have to do everything (overachievers, please be released), but we pray that the benefits of fully engaging with the material will bring joy, unity, and a deeper understanding of God's Word. Don't give up on week three after you've started your gym membership in January. Keep on (pick the book back up in March!), knowing that it can take a while for a band to find its rhythm together. Discover and use the pieces that work for you and your family.

# Learn, Grow, and Have Fun Together

"Learning happens in circles, not rows." This phrase certainly didn't start with us, but we believe it to be true, and whether it is applied at church or in your family room, there's beauty in communal growth. Lean in and ask yourself the difficult questions. You won't believe all God can do to grow you in faith and together as a family.

# The Lost Hiker and the Importance of Friends

---

*My son, do not go along with them, do not set foot on their paths; for their feet rush into evil, they are swift to shed blood.*

—PROVERBS 1:15–16

---

**When we were living** in California, we loved to take our kids on different hikes to see the amazing scenery. One summer, as school came to a close, we googled "easy hike" and found a listing for a trail that promised a beautiful waterfall. As we arrived and headed to the path, we noticed that we were walking down what was basically a very steep hill that others may have called a mountain. We kept going, thinking about the listing on Google: "easy hike." The problem was that we didn't know who had written that description; about halfway down the hill it became clear that it must have been a mountain climber. To make matters even more intense there was a search and rescue team in the area looking for a missing hiker who hadn't returned home the night before. Our daughter learned the name of the missing hiker and began helping the rescue team by calling for him, too.

Like the hiker did, it's easy to lose our way in life. We can easily be led off course by our friendships or outside influences, and what seems like a smooth, manageable path can quickly turn hazardous. This week's Bible verse reminds us that the people we spend time with have such an important role in our lives. God's Word reminds us that two are better than one, but that bad company corrupts good morals. We have to be so wise about those we spend time with in order to see the red flags that warn us of danger ahead. You might find yourself hanging out with a person who has a pattern of negativity, a distrust for authority, or dangerous habits. Try to notice those signs.

Scripture is clear to remind us of the paths that lead to goodness and blessing and the warnings that can be seen as frustrating but are God's protecting love toward us. The warning here is like a Google review in all caps, saying "Watch out, be careful, don't do what you feel like everyone else is doing!" What might not look like much at the outset is a path that has the potential to ruin your life.

# Discussion Questions

1. What characteristics do you find are most important when choosing friends?

2. What was a bad situation that you were in with a friend that God helped you out of?

3. What are some ways you can be a wise friend to the people in your life at school, at work, or in extracurricular activities?

4. At your age right now, what are signs of good or bad influences?

## Family Activity

Draw a picture of the perfect friend for you. Imagine what they might look like, what they might be wearing, and, perhaps most important, what they are doing or playing with. Write near the picture what personality traits they have and what they are interested in. Think about things you might have in common, or how your opposite traits might complement one another. Go around the family table and describe this aspirational person to one another.

## Action of the Week

Think of a friend who has helped you make wise choices. Write that person a note. You can thank them for being a good influence on you, describe how they are special to you, or encourage them if they need it. Send the note via snail mail. If you are able, include a small gift or little treat.

## Guided Prayer

God, we thank You for the gift of friendship that You created. We pray that You would bring wise friendships into each of our lives. Lord, help us divert from relationships that draw us away from You. Be Lord over each of our friendships. In Jesus's name, Amen.

# It's MINE

---

*Do nothing out of selfish ambition or vain conceit, but in humility value others above yourselves.*

—PHILIPPIANS 2:3

---

### "But it's MINE!"

This refrain often fills the air at our house, as one sibling plays the trump card of ownership. When a fight breaks out over a ball, book, treat, or game controller, the assumption is that the original owner is in charge. If they opened it under the tree at Christmas or purchased it with birthday money, they should be allowed to control what happens with it, right?

We emphasize ownership because it can be a safe way to be selfish. Our hearts want what we want when we want it. When we don't get it, we often react with anger, hurting those we love. One of our challenges as Christians is to change our mindset from "it's mine" to something healthier that places more value on others. When we can see helping others as a primary goal, healthier relationships happen.

It's natural to want to go first, be best, and get what we think is coming to us. Paul is suggesting that God wants us to not focus on what should be ours, but to see everything we have and are as opportunities to serve others. When we count our parents, grandparents, or siblings as more significant than ourselves, it becomes easier to share and be gracious with our possessions.

Notice it isn't that others are actually more important than we are; it's that we should *count* them that way. This is the way Jesus treated us in coming to Earth and going to the cross. He put our needs over His needs. When we treat our family members with value and show them that they matter, we live in the plenty of what is *ours*.

## Discussion Questions

1. Why do we naturally want our way so badly?

2. What in your life do you find it hardest to share? Why?

3. You may have heard the saying, "It's better to give than to receive," especially at Christmas. Have you experienced that?

4. Who is someone you know who excels at giving? How does that person make you feel?

### Family Activity

Pull up a YouTube clip of an Olympic 200-meter final. Mute the announcers and provide your own commentary. Instead of focusing on who is winning, aggressively and joyfully cheer for the last-place finisher (maybe even record yourself doing it). Be careful not to mock the person or their efforts; just cheer for someone who may not be getting all the glory. After all, last place is often first place in the kingdom of God.

## Action of the Week

Make a contest this week over something undesirable. Whether it's the back seat of the car or the stool at the dinner table, give a small prize or a verbal reward to whoever gets the bad spot. Training your mind to see service as godliness is the goal. The one who serves the most wins!

## Guided Prayer

God, this week help us seek to serve rather than insisting on our own way. Help us treat others as more important than ourselves. Show us that loving others is where true joy is found. Thank You, Jesus. Amen.

# Upside-Down Living

---

*But love your enemies, do good to them, and lend to them without expecting to get anything back. Then your reward will be great, and you will be children of the Most High, because He is kind to the ungrateful and wicked.*

—LUKE 6:35

---

"Economy" is a big word for the way that goods and services are made and exchanged in a certain place. Let's say you want a new video game system (parents can play, too!) and you check the company's website to see what it costs. You save your money from work, chores, allowance, etc., and once you have enough saved you go to the store and purchase that item. But if you were to travel to a different country and attempt to buy the same gaming system with the money that you saved, you wouldn't be able to do it because the currency is different. Most countries have different types of bills or coins. The same is true for God's economy.

God's economy is different from any other economy on Earth. For example, in God's economy, action has more value than words. This verse says God will reward things we wouldn't even typically do for our friends, never mind our enemies. Have you ever tried to love someone who is difficult, do good to someone who may not like you, or lend to someone without expecting anything back? It's difficult. But here's the awesome part: When we follow

Christ's example, His economy expands, and we get the opportunity to spread His love throughout the world! These instructions aren't just something Jesus was saying because He thought it was good for us to do, it's exactly what He lived out.

Have you ever tried to wrap a really big present that wouldn't fit into a bag or a box? You can go to some pretty extreme efforts. God's love for us is like that. It can't fit into a pretty box with a big, beautiful bow. But He allows us to experience that love and wants us to share it with others because there's more than enough of it to go around.

# Discussion Questions

1. What was a time when you loved someone who was difficult to love? What did God teach you through that experience?

2. How do you feel when you read that God is kind to the ungrateful and wicked?

3. How has God loved you when you were difficult to love?

4. What do you think is the most valuable currency in God's economy? Why?

## Family Activity

Make a dessert and card for someone in your family's life who might have been difficult toward you, even if you don't feel like doing it. Try to look at them through God's eyes and imagine how Jesus might see them. Deliver the gift to them as a family to show them love.

## Action of the Week

This week, when there is a person in your life who is frustrating you at work, school, or the playground, choose to stop what you are doing and pray for them.

## Guided Prayer

Thank You, God, for Your love toward us, which we can't earn and don't deserve but have anyway. Please remind us of Your all-encompassing love and help us show it to everyone we encounter this week. Help us shine Your light through the way we treat those You have put in our paths this week. In Jesus's name, Amen.

# Quick to Listen Is Quick to Joy

*My dear brothers and sisters, take note of this: Everyone should be **quick to listen,** slow to speak, and slow to become angry, because human anger does not produce the righteousness that God desires.*

—JAMES 1:19–20

**Why would James** need to tell us to be quick to listen? Surely in families we never struggle to listen, right? Our family loves to talk. It wouldn't be unusual to find all six people at our dinner table trying to tell a story at the same time. We have had to learn how frustrating it is when we talk over one another. There are three reasons why we must slow down our talking and listen to what our loved ones are saying:

**Quick to listen helps make sure we understand.**

Just because you think you understand doesn't mean you do. Active listening requires trying to understand the words being said and the heart behind them. Asking clarifying questions and quietly pondering the answers is being quick to hear.

**Quick to listen means adjusting our perspective.**

You aren't truly listening to your family members unless you are willing to adjust your perspective. No one sees the past or present with complete objectivity or clarity. If your only purpose in conversation is to close a sale with your viewpoint, you aren't actually ever listening.

**Quick to listen doesn't rush the other person.**

True listening isn't always efficient, especially for alpha personalities. Often you might even be able to finish someone else's paragraph more clearly than they can. You might think you're being helpful, but the core purpose of most conversations is connection, not information exchange. Sometimes letting someone waste a few minutes belaboring a long point is a necessary part of loving them.

When we are quick to hear, we are loving each other well and loving God well at the same time.

# Discussion Questions

1. Do you think you generally make people feel heard? When do you find it hard to listen to others?

2. What are some nonverbal cues that show someone else we are listening?

3. Have you ever had the feeling of being really listened to? What does it feel like?

4. Can you think of a time when you took the time to really listen to someone in a way you hadn't before? What was the outcome?

## Family Activity

Practice listening by looking. We miss so much communication because we are often looking at screens instead of each other. Practice looking at each other face-to-face, mouthing the words to a sentence without audibly speaking. See how many sentences you can decode properly. Then discuss how much easier it is to listen when looking directly at the person speaking.

## Action of the Week

Get an "interruption jar" and a stack of quarters. For a week, every time someone interrupts at the family table, they must put a quarter in the jar. At the end of the week, find a church or charity to give the money to.

## Guided Prayer

God, help us this week to listen well to each other. Help us not focus only on our own words, but also on those of the people we love. Thank You, Jesus. Amen.

# Slow to Speak Is Quick to Joy

*My dear brothers and sisters, take note of this: Everyone should be quick to listen, **slow to speak** and slow to become angry, because human anger does not produce the righteousness that God desires.*

—JAMES 1:19–20

**In our family,** we love to finish each other's sentences. Almost every time one of our boys tells a famous family tale, someone jumps in to loudly exclaim the punch line. The problem is, we often jump in to speak before we really finish listening. We have a bad habit of offering advice or critique or praise too quickly. This week's verse encourages us to be slow to speak to make sure we complete the transition from hearing to listening.

**Sometimes our rush to make a point keeps us from making a difference.**

Conversation is not combat. Common ground creates more good than social media–style fighting. Two people who care enough to pause and understand each other have a better chance of agreeing than two people who trade blows with perfectly sharpened facts.

**Sometimes our tone says more than our words.**

Christians are really good at saying the right words, but sometimes their tone betrays their heart. Like an elementary schooler sighing and growling "*Sorry!*" before stalking away, if our tone is aggressive or harsh, our words can be gracious and still not come close to solving the issue.

**Sometimes our need to respond diminishes our message.**
All conversations eventually end, and being willing to let someone else have the last word is often loving. The need to get the last word in or to have our perspective heard again is not a great habit. Letting someone tell you something hard to hear and then saying, "Thank you for expressing yourself" or "Can I have a little time to think about that?" is often more loving than any response (including an apology) that you can give.

By being slow to speak, we love well and promote peace in our families.

# Discussion Questions

1. What makes it hard to not jump in and interrupt when a family member is talking?

2. Have you ever felt misunderstood because you were only partially listened to?

3. Why do we find it hard to listen to people we love?

4. Think of a time when you jumped in to respond to a social media post or participate in a debate before you knew the full story. If you had known all the details going in, would your response have been different?

## Family Activity

Call a friend or extended family member. Ask them one question designed to get a long response. Listen and don't say another word. You can offer verbal agreement periodically, like "That makes sense, tell me more," but do not interrupt or change the subject. Simply see how long they answer your question before they are done talking. Try the same thing with another friend or family member. Notice how much we can miss out on due to being quick to speak. (Then call the friend back and explain the exercise.)

## Action of the Week

Don't interrupt anyone. In every conversation this week, wait until the other person is done talking before offering a response. For some temperaments, this will be very difficult, but stick with it—it's good practice!

## Guided Prayer

God, help us this week to listen first and speak slowly. Help us intentionally give our best attention to those we love so they feel heard and understood. We pray for a guard over our mouths so that they honor You. In Jesus's name, Amen.

# Mustard Seed Faith

*He replied, "Because you have so little faith. Truly I tell you, if you have faith as small as a mustard seed, you can say to this mountain, 'Move from here to there,' and it will move. Nothing will be impossible for you."*

—MATTHEW 17:20–21

**Sometimes faith seems** downright crazy. Whether you're Noah, who built a humongous boat, or Abraham, who was promised numerous descendants but whose wife couldn't have babies until she was ninety, it takes strength to trust God when you can't see the end from the beginning. Sure, Noah and Abraham have hall-of-fame faith stories, but what was their faith like when they were waiting?

Many of us have had our hopes deferred and would rather err on the side of "safe faith." What is safe faith? Essentially, it's faith with a side of plan B, or a side of doubt. But it's just like Jesus to use the smallest seed of "true faith" to yield some of the largest results. Just like the beginnings of faith, the mustard seed isn't what is impressive. It looks exactly like what it is: a start. True faith not only plants but waters, and it looks for buds with anticipation. But often in our humanness, right after we take a step of faith, doubt comes knocking at the door.

Maybe you are a risk taker who loves crazy faith stories and takes giant leaps, believing in bountiful provision from tiny seeds. Maybe you're on the other extreme and you love to play it safe. Either way, this verse reveals that God is pleased when you bring Him your measly mustard seed, especially when you muster (see what we did there?) all your courage to bring it. You can trust the same God that Sarah and Abraham and Noah did. You may not always know when you will see the ROI (return on investment) of the faith you are investing in right now, but the seeds of faith *always* produce in God's economy.

# Discussion Questions

1. Are you more likely to be a risk taker or are you a person who likes to play it safe? Why?

2. What situation do you need your faith to grow in right now? What are the doubts that make your faith difficult?

3. Has there been a time when you were able to have faith that yielded mountain-moving results? Share it with your family.

4. Look up a picture of a mustard seed and then a picture of the tree it grows into. How would you describe each one? What do you notice about the difference between the two?

## *Family Activity*

Make an obstacle course as a family. Take turns blindfolding one person and have another person guide them as they go through the obstacle course. They will have to trust their guide to give the correct instructions to make it through successfully. When the person is having doubts or feeling unsure, encourage them along! Take turns with each family member.

## Action of the Week

When feeling doubtful or unsure about something throughout the week, say to yourself and one another, "Nothing is impossible with God!" Try to encourage each member of your family with this at least once this week.

## Guided Prayer

Dear God, thank You for accepting our small seeds of faith. We know You can grow them to be greater than we can imagine. We pray that You would root out the things that are causing us to doubt and help us trust You in faith. Thank You, Jesus. Amen.

# Where the Power Is!

*Therefore, confess your sins to each other and pray for each other so that you may be healed. The prayer of a righteous person is powerful and effective.*

—JAMES 5:16

**The Bible has a lot** to say about prayer. Even people who might not believe in the Bible still believe in the power of prayer. Most people think of prayer only as the avenue to ask God for the things they want, and yes, that's one of its primary purposes. But as you grow in Christ, you come to realize that He also uses prayer to change the heart of the pray-er, revealing that the state of our heart is more important than what we "get."

1 John 5:14 says, "This is the confidence we have in approaching God: that if we ask anything according to His will, He hears us." He wants us to come to Him believing that we have already received what we have prayed for. But prayer can be so much more than petitioning God for something we want; it is a time to adore God for who He is and thank Him for what He has done for us. And, as James 5:16 suggests, it's also an opportunity to confess our sins, pray for those who have hurt us, and be reconciled with Him.

In 2016, we had a prayer series at our church where our pastor encouraged us to get on our knees and pray daily for something specific for forty days. I was shocked by what God brought from our prayer. We were praying about something that God had closed the door on a year earlier. But as we came to God on our knees in prayer, we saw Him bring an answer that to this day makes us praise His faithfulness. You may not see the end result you are hoping for today, but as you continue praying, the answers to your past prayers make great reminders of what God can do in your future.

# Discussion Questions

1. In what area of prayer do you need to grow most: adoration, confession, thanksgiving, or petition?

2. Do you struggle with believing God will answer your prayers? Why or why not?

3. Has there been a time when you saw God answer prayer in your life or someone else's that made an impact on you?

4. What do you pray about the most for yourself? What do you pray about the most for other people?

## Family Activity

Sometimes we pray for the same things over and over. To mix it up, make a "prayer jar" using a canning jar, ice pop sticks, and markers. Decorate the jar and write out things on the ice pop sticks that your family needs prayer for. Each night at dinner, have someone pick a stick and pray accordingly. Here is a list of ideas to get you started on the ice pop sticks: obedience, self-control, finances, a problem at school or work, community/government, leaders, church, forgiveness, something you need, relationship with God, reconciliation with a family member, siblings, friends, or health. Praise God for His goodness!

## Action of the Week

If you don't already know it by heart, learn the Lord's Prayer (Matthew 6:9–13 or Luke 11:2–4). Take one verse per day and talk through what it says and how you can apply it to your life.

## Guided Prayer

Dear God, thank You that we can come to the God of the universe in prayer and that You hear us. Give us confidence as we pray that You are working on our behalf. God, show us answers to prayer this week. In Jesus's name, Amen.

# Treasure

*Indeed, if you call out for insight and cry
aloud for understanding, and if you look for
it as for silver and search for it as for hidden
treasure, then you will understand the fear of
the Lord and find the knowledge of God.*

—PROVERBS 2:3–5

In 2010, a millionaire, art dealer, and author named Forrest Fenn hid a box of treasures amounting to $2 million in the Rocky Mountains. He was eighty years young when he hid the treasure box and wrote a poem with a treasure map in his self-published book *The Thrill of the Chase*. It took roughly ten years for someone to finally retrieve it, although Fenn believes more than 200,000 people tried; four people even died in the attempt.

What would you have gone through to find that treasure box? So often we will put ourselves through perilous efforts in order to find "treasure" like a bigger house, regular vacations, or social media likes without realizing that the book we already have, the Bible, has timeless truths that are true treasure. The Bible offers a multitude of examples of God's abundant love for you and His peace that brings comfort in all circumstances. And unlike Fenn's poem, which created confusion for the hikers, we can understand and gain insight into what the Bible says—if we persist in seeking it. To find treasure worth our time, we usually have to search for a while. Yet, in our insatiable, rapidly moving culture, we want to know things quickly, and if we can't find something with a mere search on the internet, we are disappointed! This week's verse reveals that when we approach God's Word, sometimes it takes time, effort, and persistence to gain practical insight we can apply to our personal lives.

Hidden treasure is rare, but we would bet that the person who found Fenn's treasure box showed all their friends and probably didn't let it out of their sight. If we can value God's Word that highly, God will continue to reveal new things to each of us and encourage us with the treasure we so badly need.

# Discussion Questions

1.  Would you have wanted to set out on the journey to find the treasure that Fenn hid? Why or why not?

2.  What is something you don't understand about God's Word and would like clarity from God about?

3.  What Bible verse has been a treasure for you that you go to when you feel unsure or are having a difficult time?

4.  What do you think is a treasure the world values that God might not? Why do you think it takes so long to reach God's treasure?

## Family Activity

Split up into two teams. Have each team create a treasure map with an accompanying poem for something valuable in the home. Then swap your maps and poems and have the other team try to find your treasure. Take one night to create the treasure maps and one night to try to find the treasure.

## Action of the Week

Read through one Psalm each day this week and find a verse that your family can hold on to as "treasure" in difficult times. Post this verse somewhere you all will see it so that it becomes treasure to you.

## Guided Prayer

Dear God, we thank You for Your Word, which is more precious than silver or gold. Help us not only to try to locate treasure in this world but also to seek You for guidance when we don't understand scripture or when we are trying to apply it to our lives. Help us to have the right perspective when it comes to You and Your Word. In Jesus's name, Amen.

# The Bridge of Love

---

*For God so loved the world that he gave his
one and only Son, that whoever believes in
Him shall not perish but have eternal life.
For God did not send His Son into the
world to condemn the world, but to save
the world through Him.*

—JOHN 3:16–17

---

**In Palos Verdes,** California, there is a beautiful hike
that allows you to climb down the cliffs alongside the
Pacific. You begin on a long trail that leads to the cliff's
edge, and almost out of nowhere you can see an expanse
of the Pacific Ocean that truly takes your breath away.
Farther down the trail, a bridge stretches between two
cliffs that otherwise wouldn't join. Once you walk across
the bridge, you zig and zag down gravel trails in order to
sit at the bank of the Pacific. The quietness and serenity
that meets you is heavenly.

The bridge is a beautiful symbol of what Jesus did for
us. Since we were young children, we have all chosen to
sin. Since Adam and Eve sinned in the garden, sin has
required a payment. In the Old Testament, people sacrifice animals to atone for their sin. In the New Testament,
Jesus Himself becomes the sacrifice for our sin. When we
believe in Him, we don't have to die because of our sin;
we can spend eternity with Him. Like the bridge on the
cliff, God built a bridge for us through the cross. Our sin
used to separate us from Him, but He made a way for us

to experience His love in the here and now, as well as in eternity. Had he left us to our own devices, we would be stuck on a figurative cliff, without a path or bridge. And although we can know about the ocean by seeing pictures of its expanse, there's a difference between knowing about it and experiencing it. In the same way, knowing about God's love because you have accepted it, believed it in your heart, and confessed your sin allows you to experience its fullness. Jesus made a way because He didn't want anyone to perish. Today is a great day to accept that truth in your heart.

## Discussion Questions

1. When was the first time you heard about Jesus and His love for you?

2. Can you tell about a specific time when you accepted Jesus as your Lord and savior? If you haven't, do you want to pray for that today?

3. What is keeping you from accepting Jesus as your savior?

4. What is your favorite part about John 3:16–17? Why? Share with your family.

## Family Activity

Have everyone share the story of the time that they first heard of God's love for them. What was their experience and how did it make them feel? Pray for each family member to have the opportunity to share their story or invite someone to church to hear about God's love for them.

## Action of the Week

Think about accepting God's gift for you and thank God for it. If you have already accepted it, make a list of people you know who don't know Jesus and pray for them. Keep the list with you for a week and ask God to show Himself to them.

## Guided Prayer

Dear God, thank You for Your love. Thank You for seeing that our sin separated us from You, and for making a way for us so we can know Your love and spend eternity with You. We believe that You died for our sins and that You are Lord. We confess that we are sinners in need of a savior—and we accept You as our savior. Praise You, Jesus. Amen!

# Fear the Right Thing

*There is no fear in love. But perfect love casts out fear, because fear has to do with punishment. The one who fears is not made perfect in love.*

—1 JOHN 4:18

**Every so often** one of our boys will come downstairs to our bedroom and wake us from sleep with a problem: "I had a bad dream." Often they don't know many more details than that, but they are awake and uneasy. One of us gets out of bed and walks them over to the couch outside our room, lays a blanket over them, and says a quick prayer with them before going back to bed. As of this writing, the kids have never failed to go right back to sleep. In the future that may change, but so far, so good.

Why?

Because in those moments, being reminded that our protection is close pushes fear of the dream away. Being reminded of a loving parent close by focuses attention on safety rather than concern. As a family, we crave safety. When someone we trust points us to it, we usually believe them and trust it. Our trust in those we love helps keep fear away.

But there are way scarier things in this life than a bad dream, right?

We do our best as families to love one another perfectly, but we often fail. We say harsh things, we act unkindly, and sometimes, without meaning to, we hurt one another. The perfect love of Jesus Christ can meet us in our fears because He isn't flawed and frail like we are.

When we remember the love God has for us, our fear tends to melt away. That doesn't mean a new school, new city, or change in living situation isn't difficult, it means we trust something bigger. John is telling us that God's perfect love is bigger than any of our fears.

So don't be afraid. Not because we know what the future holds, but because we know Who holds the future.

# Discussion Questions

1. Do you like horror movies? Why or why not?

2. When were you most scared in your life? How did you handle it?

3. Why do bad dreams bother us so much?

4. The Bible says when we're afraid it's because we fear "punishment," or the negative consequences of something. What might your life be like if negative consequences never bothered you? How would things be different if we always trusted God that much?

## Family Activity

Have everyone get out a piece of paper along with markers or crayons. Draw the scariest monster you possibly can. Add horns or big teeth or wings, whatever makes it seem scariest. Then discuss as a family why you drew the monster the way you did and what about it makes it especially scary to you, and maybe what that reveals about what you naturally fear.

## Action of the Week

Practice a mantra of faith. Anytime you find yourself in a scary situation, say out loud, "I don't have to be afraid of this, because Jesus loves me and is with me." Watch how, slowly but surely, your feelings meet those words.

## Guided Prayer

Dear Lord, today help us let Your perfect love cast out our fear. Help our family be strong and courageous because of Your love. Thank You, Jesus. We pray in Your name, Amen.

# Waiting Always Wins

*The waters flooded the earth for a hundred and fifty days.*

—GENESIS 7:24

*But God remembered Noah.*

—GENESIS 8:1

**While we were growing up** in suburban Chicago, there was something about those afternoons in the spring that felt never-ending. After the long winter, on a warm day, it felt like the clock moved so slowly and school would never end. We wanted so badly to get outside and play, and the process of trying to wait felt miserable. Ever feel like that?

Noah spent a lot of time waiting, too: First, he waited for what many believe to have been around seventy-five years while he built the ark, hoping he'd heard God's voice clearly. Then Noah waited for about a year on the ark, watching the world as he knew it be destroyed. Then he waited during the weekly checking of the ground to see if the flood was almost gone. Was he ever going to get off that boat?

Waiting stinks if we see it as wasted time. But what if . . . it's *appointed* time, as the Bible refers to a time that was decided on in advance? How would your daily schedule and outlook right now be different if you believed God had a supernatural purpose for you in the time you were waiting? All through the Bible, God does great things through those who are forced to wait.

You may be doing your part and not seeing results yet, whether it's getting a degree, making a certain team, a promotion at work, or the end of a school year. You may be barely holding on, but you *are* still holding on. God may seem silent, but He's still working, so keep waiting. Because God *always* ultimately blesses obedience, keep on waiting. God hasn't forgotten. Your waiting will end. And when it finally ends, you want to be proud of how you waited.

# Discussion Questions

1. Have you ever felt like you couldn't possibly wait anymore?

2. Why does waiting seem to make the time pass more slowly?

3. It can be tough to wait. How can we make better use of the times when we are waiting?

4. Have you ever waited for something and seen God come through?

## *Family Activity*

Bring out a favorite treat—cookies or cupcakes, something everyone in the family loves. Put one on a plate in front of you, but don't eat it. For two minutes, just look at it. Then for two more minutes, smell it, but don't taste it. Then for two additional minutes, describe what it will taste like.

Then eat. Discuss what the time of anticipation felt like, both good and bad.

## Action of the Week

Take note of every time you feel impatient this week. Keep a little list, whether mentally or on a notepad or phone. What seems to make you the most impatient? Try to see patterns that reveal why you don't want to wait.

## Guided Prayer

Dear Lord, help us trust that while we are waiting, You are working. Help us believe You more, and give us Your patience. Thank You, Jesus. Amen.

# The Power of Release

*Then he fell on his knees and cried out, "Lord,
do not hold this sin against them." When he
had said this, he fell asleep.*

—ACTS 7:60

**Our verse for this week** takes place at a particularly dramatic moment. Stephen, a deacon of the early church, is filled with the Holy Spirit, and he is not willing to turn his back on Jesus. Because of the anger of religious leaders around him, he is being killed for his faith. And yet, in his last moments, He is pleading with God to have mercy on the people *throwing rocks at him.*

In families, we so easily become victims of our victimhood. We hold grudges about broken video game controllers, stains on the couch, and who got to sit in the front seat. We ponder every little frustration while building spiritual-sounding reasons for our brutality. Unfortunately, Christian folks can sometimes be the most unkind to each other.

Yet, Stephen is able to care for those who are killing him unjustly. In the last moment of his life, he begs God not to give them what they deserve. That's mercy. Although they deserve to have Stephen curse them for their unfair treatment, he asks God to spare them.

Often our families suffer because we refuse to release each other. We hold on to the grudges and offenses, letting them build up over time. Very little that happens to us could be as big as what Stephen asks God to forgive, yet we often keep records of wrongs, punishing each other for mistakes. But we are rarely happier after we list all the mistakes another has made.

What if the secret to more joy in our families is more mercy for each other's mistakes? Rather than punishing or keeping a list of mistakes, imagine how much joy would come our way if we let things go.

# Discussion Questions

1. Why do we often want others to be punished for their mistakes rather than have mercy extended to them?

2. When you make a mistake, do you want mercy or justice?

3. Have you ever been shown mercy when you needed it after a big mistake?

4. If yes, what did it feel like to be released from your mistake?

## *Family Activity*

Gather small slips of paper and a burning candle. Write down any situation you can think of where someone hurt you. If you can think of it and it still bothers you, go ahead and write it down. You can share what you are writing or keep it private. Slowly and safely, use the candle to burn the paper. You can also use a fireplace or a fire pit, if you have access to one. As the paper burns, ask God to give you the mercy to let go of the offenses of others.

## Action of the Week

Use this question as a mantra: "What would mercy do?" Try in every situation, whether joyful or frustrating, to pause before responding, and ask yourself what mercy would do. How would you treat someone if you were choosing to be merciful? What would it be like to release someone from punishment or resentment? Then act accordingly.

## Guided Prayer

Dear Lord, help us be people of mercy, not penalizing or punishing others, but blessing them. Remind us to treat others mercifully, rather than brutally. Thank You for the times we have been shown mercy. Help us, Jesus. Amen.

# Sloth versus Ant

*Go to the ant, you sluggard; consider its ways and be wise! It has no commander, no overseer, or ruler, yet it stores provisions in summer and gathers its food at harvest. How long will you lie there, you sluggard? When will you get up from your sleep?*

—PROVERBS 6:6–9

**Did you know** that ants live on every continent on Earth except for . . . wait for it . . . ANTarctica? It's true! Ants are annoying as heck if you are attempting to get them out of your home, but they're fascinating creatures when you look at their industrious nature. Did you know that ants can carry up to fifty times their body weight? Proverbs says they exemplify the way of wisdom because of their diligence in work. Ants don't need convincing; they get to work without being asked and they work tirelessly. Furthermore, the ant doesn't just think about the here and now, it stores up provisions for the future.

This passage contrasts the ant and the "sluggard," who might be defined as a habitually lazy person, kind of like the sloth from the movie *Zootopia*. Cute as he may be, the sloth in that movie is slow and lazy even at his workplace. Proverbs teaches that this kind of laziness can actually lead to unrighteousness (a big word meaning "ungodliness"), whereas the way of wisdom is diligence. This doesn't mean you can't ever rest or relax when you need to! But in general, whether you are at work or at home, when you're putting effort toward an instrument, a sport, or a household chore, your willingness to put in hard work matters to God. In all that we do, we are representing God, and we can use those opportunities to shine a light on our relationship with God and work tirelessly for His kingdom.

God's use of a creature as small and unimpressive as an ant to represent qualities he wants us to follow reminds us that the kingdom of God is upside down from most of the ways we look at things. But His way is best, and although you may be as cute as a sloth, we should all set out to work like ants!

# Discussion Questions:

1. By nature, are you more like the ant who likes to work or are you more like the sluggard who likes to lay around?

2. What is an area you have put a lot of effort and work into where you feel like your diligence paid off?

3. Are there any areas where you feel you could work harder?

4. What are some steps you can take this week to become more diligent and hardworking?

## Family Activity

As a family, make a plan to serve your community. Work diligently to clean up garbage on your street or another road near your home, rake your neighbor's leaves, or volunteer at a local food pantry. Work hard together to serve the kingdom, not for your benefit but for the benefit of others.

## Action of the Week

Set a goal to put in fifteen minutes a day helping your family clean and organize your house. Make a list as a family of things around the house that need to be done and assign chores in any way that works for you. See how a little bit of work each day adds up to much accomplishment.

## Guided Prayer

Dear God, we thank You for the example of the industrious ant. We ask for diligence where we would otherwise choose laziness. We ask for persistence when we want to give up. God, help us grow in these ways so that we can serve Your kingdom well. In Jesus's name, Amen.

# Since the Garden . . .

*No temptation has overtaken you except
what is common to mankind. And God is
faithful; He will not let you be tempted
beyond what you can bear. But when you are
tempted, He will also provide a way out so
that you can endure it.*

—1 CORINTHIANS 10:13

**We have a fake cake** that sits on our island
counter in the kitchen. The piping and icing are precise
and the strawberries that sit on top look delectable. Often
people will say, "Look at that cake! Can I have a piece?"
Their disappointment and disapproval are universal when
they're met with "It's just for decoration!"

The truth is that if we had a real cake on a pedestal in
our kitchen, it wouldn't last a week! Between our four kids
and ourselves—a sliver here, a lick there—no one would be
able to resist it. Often this is what sin feels like in our lives.
It's placed right in front of us, and we notice it. This births
desire, and we wonder if we can have some of it without
anyone finding out.

Since the Garden of Eden, humankind has been
tempted by power, pleasure, and position. Jesus Himself is
tempted by the devil in the wilderness. He is hungry and
alone, and the devil tries to tempt Him with what he would
have been attracted to himself. But Jesus, being fully man
and fully God, is able to withstand the urge and keep His
purpose and His mission in mind.

The Bible reminds us that temptation isn't an "if" experience but a "when" experience. We're going to encounter it at some point. Like Jesus, we have to know our purpose and have a plan so we don't get derailed when temptation arises. Our most powerful tool against temptation is listening to the still, small voice of the Holy Spirit, especially through calling out in prayer in moments when we feel ourselves wanting to choose pleasure over wisdom. We have to be willing to have courage no matter what the temptation is, and we must have words and actions ready in order to run from moments when we feel ourselves giving in to saying something we shouldn't or eating something we've been told not to.

# Discussion Questions

1. What is a temptation you have experienced in the last week? How did you handle it? How can you prepare for it if it happens again?

2. Out of power (being in charge of something), pleasure (something you enjoy doing), or position (feeling important), what tempts you most frequently?

3. The Bible says God "will provide a way out" when we are tempted. Have you ever been in a situation where you felt God help you resist temptation?

4. In Matthew 4:1–11, the story of Jesus being tempted in the wilderness, Jesus resists each temptation by quoting scripture. Can you find a Bible verse that will help you when one of your temptations shows up?

## Family Activity

This week, have a meal that you fast from (skip altogether) as a family. As you fast, pray together about a specific sin you feel tempted by. If you feel comfortable sharing your sins with your family, you can pray for one another as you fast. Break the fast by taking your next meal together and sharing what you learned, if anything, through fasting.

## Action of the Week

Spend five minutes each day praying for the specific temptations each family member is facing and for them to be able to withstand the pressure to give in to temptation. Ask God to provide them with a "way out," as the verse promises, and thank Him for His faithfulness to each of you.

## Guided Prayer

Thank You, God, for Your faithfulness and for providing a way out when we are tempted. We pray for a fresh desire to fight temptation, the courage to resist the enemy's tactics, and the words and actions we need to overcome whatever we face. In Jesus's name, Amen.

# You Only Live Twice

*"What no eye has seen, what no ear has heard, and what no human mind has conceived"—the things God has prepared for those who love Him.*

—1 CORINTHIANS 2:9

**"YOLO" was a phrase** that was popular a few years ago. It is an acronym for "You only live once," and most people took that as agency to proceed with whatever pleasure would make them happy at the time. During that time, we were planning a winter retreat, and we called it "YOLT," reframing YOLO into the reality that, in actuality, "You only live twice." The reminder for students and leaders alike is that we shouldn't just seize the moment in the day-to-day, but we should instead live this life with our eyes toward eternity, living life the right way—with some self-restraint—to make sure we get to Heaven. The hope of Heaven is real, and unlike most things here on Earth, our expectations will only be exceeded there!

The greatest gift in knowing Jesus is that He loved us so much He was willing to sacrifice His life on our behalf so that we could spend eternity with Him. Heaven isn't some idyllic hope, it's as real as the shoes on your feet and the headband in your hair. You can anticipate it as your eternal destination with confidence and peace when you know Jesus Christ as your savior. We don't have to be scared about death. In the Gospels, Jesus tells us that He is going to prepare a place for us and that His father's house has many rooms. In the book of Revelation, John writes that the streets will be made of pure gold! Can you even imagine that? The Bible says that Heaven will be populated by a great multitude of people from every nation and language. Worship will be next-level as we all sing to Him. He also promises to transform our bodies to be like His glorified body, and that any work we have done for His kingdom will be rewarded there. We can look forward to Heaven because all things will be made right, and there will be no tears, no pain, and no more death. The things that hinder us on this side of Heaven will be no more, and our new life in Christ will be far greater than we could imagine here on Earth.

# Discussion Questions

1. What do you find most exciting about Heaven? What are some things you hope Heaven will have that aren't mentioned in the Bible?

2. Do you fear death? If so, how does learning about Heaven calm some of those fears?

3. What do you struggle with on Earth that you look forward to being different in Heaven?

4. What is your favorite verse in the Bible about Heaven? Why?

## Family Activity

Play the Heaven/Not in Heaven game! You will need two baskets, one labeled "Heaven" and one labeled "Not in Heaven." On index cards or small pieces of paper, write down some things that will be in Heaven and some that won't. Divide the cards so that each person in the family gets to place a few in each basket. Then review the answers. In the "Heaven" basket, you might include things like laughter, hugs, love, friends, family, God, Jesus, angels, plants, happiness, gold, fun, houses, beauty, perfection, peace, learning, games, singing, or dancing. In "Not in Heaven," you might have: Satan, hate, lies, loneliness, jealousy, sin, anger, death, sickness, sadness, earthquakes, floods, ugliness, greed, boredom, fear, medicine, or war. Let this game reinforce how many amazing things God has stored up for us in Heaven.

## Action of the Week

Have everyone write down questions they have about Heaven and try to find answers together this week through looking at books, searching online, reading the Bible, or even asking your pastor.

## Guided Prayer

Thank You, God, for the hope we have of Heaven being our eternal destination. Thank You for loving us enough to prepare a place for us. We pray that You would calm any fears that we have about death. In Jesus's name, Amen.

# Peace Follows Prayer

*Do not be anxious about anything, but in every situation, by prayer and petition, with thanksgiving, present your requests to God. And the peace of God, which transcends all understanding, will guard your hearts and your minds in Christ Jesus.*

—PHILIPPIANS 4:6-7

**In Acts 16,** Paul and Silas command evil spirits out of a fortune teller while preaching the gospel in Macedonia. When her owners realize they can no longer make money from her, they have Paul and Silas beaten and thrown in prison. This would be enough to terrify any of us. But Acts 16:25 says, "About midnight Paul and Silas were praying and singing hymns to God, and the other prisoners were listening to them." So, when Paul tells us not to be anxious but to bring our requests to God, he shares this from a place of authority. These aren't mere words for him. In prison, during one of his darkest hours, rather than choosing anxiety or fear or anger, he pursued prayer, and therefore peace.

We all face anxiety from time to time. It can paralyze us and confuse our minds, making it hard to make a wise decision. But God knows that the greatest antagonist of anxiety is trust. When we bring our torn hearts to God, we shift from fear to trusting that He will work brings us peace.

Sometimes prayer can feel intimidating, but in any strong relationship, you would share your greatest joys and your deepest concerns; your relationship with God is no different. Notice that Paul doesn't tell us to pray polite prayers but to honestly present our requests to God. Think about it: You are bringing your requests to the creator of the universe! He is the one who neither sleeps nor slumbers; only He can compel us to gratefulness and thanksgiving. Not only that, but God doesn't just receive your requests; He guards your heart and mind just like a moat guards a castle. So, bring your requests to Him just as you would a trusted friend, and you will find that releasing those burdens to Him will bring much peace and rest.

# Discussion Questions

1. What makes you the most anxious?

2. What prevents you from bringing your requests to God?

3. Has there been a time in your life when you were anxious but God brought you peace? Was it through prayer or something else?

4. Paul and Silas sing hymns to God in prison. Is there a song you have sung in the midst of fear or anxiety? How has it helped you? Share it with your family.

## Family Activity

Build a fortress together. Use Legos, magnetic tiles, or another material of your choice to build a tower and then a moat around it. Work together to make the structure as solid as you can. Use this as an opportunity to remember how God guards our hearts and minds in Christ Jesus when we bring our requests to Him.

## Action of the Week

When feeling anxious this week, follow this prayer pattern: (1) bring requests, (2) give thanks, and (3) ask for peace. Report back to the family at the end of each day on what happens when you come to God in prayer.

## Guided Prayer

Dear God, thank You for allowing us the opportunity to talk to You through prayer, and thank You for bringing peace to our anxious hearts. Thank You for hearing requests and guarding our hearts and minds in whatever we are facing. We trust You and only You. In Jesus's name, Amen.

# Use Your Gift

> *Do not neglect your gift, which was given*
> *you through prophecy when the body of*
> *elders laid their hands on you. Be diligent*
> *in these matters; give yourself wholly*
> *to them, so that everyone may see your*
> *progress.*
>
> —1 TIMOTHY 4:14–15

**It's time to get in the game.**

Whether it's because of the COVID-19 virus, being personally hurt by the church, a busy season with kids, or grief over a deep loss, it's sometimes hard to contribute much to our church communities. Maybe you've attended services or given a check, but have you been using your gifts to build the kingdom of God?

Maybe you've continued to serve out of habit, checking off the faithfulness box but not growing, expanding, or trying to make things better.

**It's time to get in the game.**

In the verses above, it isn't totally clear why Paul is insistent on pushing Timothy this way. We don't know that Timothy has a lazy spirit, so perhaps Paul is simply making sure the expectation is clear: If you have a gift, you must use it.

If God has given you something, even if it feels like it hasn't always been fruitful in the past, you must use it.

**It's time to get in the game.**

We have known some people with incredible natural singing voices. They often came to a point where they didn't want to sing anymore and wanted to do other things, like developing a teaching or counseling ministry, because singing seemed too easy. They still loved using their singing gift, but it felt cheap because it was a mostly natural. Inevitably a few years later, they'd return to singing, a little chagrined at the detour. They had lost sight of the fact that anything we have, whether natural or developed, is still a gift from God, and it pleases Him when we use it.

**It's time to get in the game.**

Be bold in how you use your gifts. Register for some new classes, go out for coffee with someone new, try a new church, or join a new group. Look for places you might be needed and new ways you can serve God. Things are difficult all around us, and we don't have the luxury of keeping our gifts hidden. We have reached a time where if we aren't using what God has gifted us, we aren't living our faith in the way God intended. Using our gifts can inspire others to use theirs as well.

# Discussion Questions

1. Does anyone in the family have a gift you admire?

2. Do you have any talents or gifts you struggle to want to use? Why is it difficult for you to use them?

3. What do you think is your strongest God-given gift? How have you used it so far?

4. What are some reasons we sometimes hide our talents?

## Family Activity

Have a family talent show. Everyone must participate—sing a song, do a dance, or tell a joke, whether it's good or not. The point is to try and to celebrate one another. Don't be passive; you must sell your act with gusto and enthusiasm. Have fun with it. Enjoy the feeling of not overthinking, but instead being overjoyed.

## Action of the Week

Look for new opportunities. It can be easy to keep using our gifts in similar ways over time. For the next week, watch intently and pray for one new way to use your gifts. Look for a unique way to use what God has given you to bless others.

## Guided Prayer

Dear Lord, help us not get distracted by disappointments. Help us keep pursuing our goals, because You gave us every one of our talents and gifts. Thank You, Jesus. Amen.

# The Opposite Game, Not the Copy Game

*A gentle answer turns away wrath, but a harsh word stirs up anger.*

—PROVERBS 15:1

Somewhere around late preschool age, kids often play a couple of the same games. In the "copy" game, they find great laughter in listening to what an adult or another kid says, then repeating it back in a funny way. The game always reaches its apex when the person being copied notices and says something like, "Hey, are you just repeating whatever I say?"

They also tend to play the opposite game, which reverses everything: cold is hot, black is white, etc. Schools often have days like this, too, where pancakes are served for lunch or clothes are worn inside out.

The concepts of these games can help us. When situations escalate, our instinct is often to fight fire with fire, to match the intense emotions of someone else with something intense of our own. Yet this week's verse suggests the opposite approach. In heightened situations, we want to bring the calm, not copy others. When we speak with aggression, problems often ratchet up and get bigger. When we can be still, problems tend to dissipate. Why?

Soft answers turn away the wrath of a sister or boss or teacher or dad because a calm response in conflict is a reminder of humanity rather than a problem to be frustrated about. We love our family members, but when they frustrate us, we can see only the problem, not the person. When we turn the emotion down, our humanity comes out, bringing a more positive outcome.

Rather than the copy game, play the opposite game, and watch your relationships get smoother.

# Discussion Questions

1. What in your family makes you the angriest?

2. What does anger feel like in your body?

3. Why is it so hard not to fight back when people make us angry?

4. What is one word or phrase you can say to bring calm to a heightened situation?

## Family Activity

Choose a favorite family movie scene or YouTube video. Have two people act it out, with one yelling their lines and the other talking very quietly but not whispering. Use the inevitable humor to discuss the power of tone of voice. What effect does each person's tone have on the other's?

## Action of the Week

Go a whole twenty-four-hour day without yelling or raising your voice for any reason, no matter what. Keep a tally of any mess-ups and report them to the family at the next family meal.

## Guided Prayer

God, this week help us stay calm in frustrating situations and make them better, not worse, with our words. Help us answer gently, not emotionally. Help us respond well. Thank You, Jesus. Amen.

# Express Yourself

*"They are the sons God has given me here,"
Joseph said to his father. Then Israel said,
"Bring them to me so I may bless them." Now
Israel's eyes were failing because of old age,
and he could hardly see. So Joseph brought
his sons close to him, and his father kissed
them and embraced them.*

—GENESIS 48:9–10

**"Are we hugging?"** We asked that question so many times as we returned to in-person church services during the COVID-19 pandemic. In the environment we were in at the time, we all loved to hug everyone, from elderly couples to young kids. There was a culture of physical touch and verbal affirmation. As we returned to physical interaction after distancing for several months, people were uncertain about how to balance their desire for physical safety with the blessing that comes from healthy touch.

Using ourselves to both verbally and physically bless those we love is an integral part of being a healthy family. Scientific studies show again and again that physical touch from those we trust communicates love in a transformative way.

Joseph had a tumultuous family life, to say the least. His brothers physically harmed him and sold him into slavery. His father's favoritism toward him negatively affected the whole family. Decades later, Joseph found a path to forgiveness, and the family was restored. We need the fuel that family blessing provides us, and physical affection is a huge part of that.

Some concepts of masculinity would see the physical affection displayed by Jacob (Israel), the grandfather, as less manly. Some may use excessive caution against abuse (necessary though that caution is) to avoid physical affection altogether. Sometimes we turn off this blessing to one another due to disappointments we have experienced. These are all traps.

Part of loving our family well is physically expressing that love. Don't let uncertainty or awkwardness keep you from giving what the people around you need in order to be blessed.

# Discussion Questions

1. Who in your family is the most naturally affectionate?

2. Do you ever find it difficult to verbally or physically express affection to your loved ones?

3. Which way do you prefer to show affection to others—through hugs or compliments? Which way do you like to receive affection best?

4. Why do you think Jesus is so often pictured in close physical proximity to those He was ministering to?

## Family Activity

Participate in one minute of praise. Make a list of all the things you love about each person at the table. Read the list while you hug the person you are speaking about. Try to go one whole minute of offering verbal and physical affirmation combined. You will be tempted to laugh, but instead try to receive the blessing. You'll be glad you did!

## Action of the Week

Check in with a positive. For one week, say something complimentary or kind to each family member every time you see them. Before leaving for the day in the morning and after returning in the afternoon, spread positive kindness into every interaction. Don't let it devolve into joking, but genuinely affirm one another.

## Guided Prayer

Dear Lord, help us express our love fully and joyfully to one another. Do not let our hurts or disappointments hinder us. Help us use ourselves fully to bless one another, as You did for us. In Jesus's name, Amen.

# Breadcrumbs

*Boaz replied, "I've been told all about what*
*you have done for your mother-in-law since*
*the death of your husband—how you left your*
*father and mother and your homeland and*
*came to live with a people you did not know*
*before. May the Lord repay you for what*
*you have done. May you be richly rewarded*
*by the Lord, the God of Israel, under whose*
*wings you have come to take refuge."*

—RUTH 2:11–12

**In the Old Testament,** we find a story about two women named Naomi and Ruth. Naomi's husband Elimelek and both her sons have passed away, leaving her and her daughters-in-law widows—all while their land is experiencing a famine. No one would choose these circumstances. Naomi is so frustrated that life doesn't look like she thinks it should that she tells her friends to call her "Mara," which means "bitter," because she feels like God has dealt bitterly with her.

Naomi tells her daughters-in-law she has nothing left to offer them and that they should go back to their families of origin. One daughter-in-law, Ruth, promises Naomi she will stay by her side. To help provide for them both, Ruth goes to work gathering leftover grain that harvesters have left in the fields. God in His kindness sends along Boaz, a relative of Naomi's late husband who allows Ruth to gather grain for Naomi and herself rather than grasping at the scraps others have left behind. Boaz reminds Ruth that God has seen what she is going through and says that because she has shown loyalty to Naomi and trusted and pursued God in her difficulty, God will repay and bless her for her obedience.

Often when we are waiting for a miracle moment, we miss the small supernatural kindnesses God is showing us all the time. Ruth exemplifies having eyes to see these "breadcrumbs"—a trail leading back to God's divine plan for her life. Her provision looks like an unexpected supply of food, a husband (Boaz), and eventually a child. God's provision usually ends up being abundantly more than we could ask for or imagine; that son ends up in the lineage of David, which makes him an ancestor of Jesus.

# Discussion Questions

1. Have you ever felt like God has dealt bitterly with you? Did He give you any breadcrumbs to show He was working even in the midst of difficulty? Share with your family.

2. Other than God, what do you run to as a refuge in the midst of disappointment?

3. What provision have you seen God bring that was better than you could have expected?

4. Ruth leaves her homeland to stay with Naomi and provide for her. Have you ever had to leave someplace comfortable and familiar to do something you knew was the better choice?

## Family Activity

Have a family conversation about real-life disappointments you may face and talk through how you can respond when they inevitably come. For example:

What should I do when . . .

- I don't make the team?

- My friend leaves me out?

- I lose something important to me?

- I don't get what I want?

- My health or an injury keeps me from something I really want to do or be?

Get advice from other family members who have gone through similar situations. Then share any experiences you've had where something good came out of a disappointment.

## Action of the Week

Look up verses about God as your refuge. Write them out on sticky notes and place them around your house to remind yourselves to look to God as your refuge amid disappointment and difficulty.

## Guided Prayer

Dear God, help us trust You in the midst of difficulty and remember that You can bring good out of the hard moments in our lives. We pray that You will give us eyes to see the breadcrumbs You've given us. In Jesus's name, Amen.

# No More Excuses

---

*Moses said to the Lord, "Pardon your servant,*
*Lord. I have never been eloquent, neither in*
*the past nor since you have spoken to your*
*servant. I am slow of speech and tongue."*
*The Lord said to him, "Who gave human*
*beings their mouths? Who makes them deaf*
*or mute? Who gives them sight or makes*
*them blind? Is it not I, the Lord?"*

—EXODUS 4:10–11

---

**Moses has one** of the most epic calls to ministry
ever. He is tending to his father-in-law's sheep when all of
a sudden, he sees a bush that is burning but isn't falling
into a heap of ash. He goes to see what is happening, and
it's the God of Heaven and Earth talking to him. God tells
Moses that He wants him to lead His people out of Egypt
and into the land He has promised them.

Some people might see this as an opportunity for their
fifteen minutes of fame, but Moses sees it as an opportunity to tell God why he shouldn't do it. First, he can't
believe God would want him! Moses might be happy to be
on the team but for sure does not want to be the captain.
But who God calls, He equips. When Moses realizes that
excuses won't deter God, he jumps headfirst into the pitfall
of not wanting to be embarrassed. Again, God reminds him
that He has the power to move the people's hearts. But
like many of us who become convinced that our reasons

why we shouldn't do something are better than God's reasons why we should, Moses is reminded of God's power. God turns Moses's staff into a serpent and brings leprosy to his hand and then restores it—you know, just another average day.

Often we, like Moses, have a desire to be right rather than brave. We think we can cleverly pull out the trump card of "Send someone else!" But God reminds us that He purposefully picks the one who isn't confident in their abilities, who will look to Him in all things instead.

# Discussion Questions

1. What is the most common excuse you make to get out of doing something?

2. Is there something God is leading you to do that you're afraid of? Is there an insecurity you have that would make you want to say no to God?

3. Why do you think God calls Moses with a burning bush? How does God most often get your attention?

4. Read Exodus 3 and 4 together as a family. What is most surprising to you about the interaction between Moses and God?

## Family Activity

Read through Exodus 3 and 4 (if you haven't already) and act out the story together. Put on some costumes and assign roles to one another. If you have time, make props like a burning bush, a staff, and a serpent. Every time Moses makes an excuse, have everyone in the family say collectively, "Send someone else!" This will help the story come alive and allow the whole family to be reminded of the power of God at work, no matter what excuses or insecurities we bring to Him.

## Action of the Week

Turn your excuses into motivation. When you don't like something, ask yourself or one another *how you can change it or impact it to be different.* Try to change your thinking. Instead of complaining, come up with actions or adjust your attitude to make things better around you.

## Guided Prayer

Dear God, thank You that You can see through our excuses and insecurities. Help us be willing to move past our fear and do what You want us to. Thank You for providing all we need to do Your will, especially when we feel unsure. In Jesus's name, Amen.

# The Maturity of Optimism

*And He said: "Truly I tell you, unless you change and become like little children, you will never enter the kingdom of Heaven."*

—MATTHEW 18:3

**The idea of change** is so exciting, whether it's a couple coming to the altar, the promises of a newly elected politician, or the dreams of a graduate going out into the world. As life progresses, the newness tends to wear off. Those newlyweds start to bicker, the legislation doesn't pass, our dreams don't come to fruition—and it's easy to become pessimistic.

Jesus refers to a lot of things when he calls us to "become like little children," but perhaps one of the deepest and most important of these is optimism. Children tend to believe what people tell them. They believe in good and see the future as bright. Their simple mentality magnifies positivity.

It's easy to see the negative and focus on what's unfair. To avoid getting hurt again, we focus on how unlikely progress is. We're so reluctant to be hopeful that it can be trendier to be annoyed by idealism than aim for it. Some Christians look at positive thinking as immature. They feel that those who really understand the world should focus on sin and problems and try to fix them. Although there's nothing wrong with a realistic outlook, pursuing positivity demonstrates wisdom. What if we could see with crystal clarity what's broken and still focus on the good? Families are healthier when they allow the positive view of the younger folks to influence the cynicism of the older ones. Jesus said it clearly: The elders have lots to learn from the youth.

# Discussion Questions

1. Who is the most naturally positive person in your family? What are some ways they handle difficult situations?

2. Why do you think it is so easy to focus on the negative?

3. What qualities of little children do you think Jesus had in mind when he encouraged adults to be like them?

4. What encourages you when you feel stuck in negative thoughts? How do you handle them?

## *Family Activity*

Play a "Find the Good" game. Have one family member bring up a current scenario (whether it's a news story or something personal) and challenge another person to find something positive in it. Take turns practicing seeing something potentially positive. Don't feel you have to justify the whole situation if it isn't a good one, but no matter how negative the circumstance, if you look with the right eyes, you can find something good.

## Action of the Week

Try to go a week without a critical assessment of anything. Choose to only speak positive words to one another. Don't take advantage by doing something wrong purposely, but be kind to one another, leaning into the power of seeing good.

## Guided Prayer

God, this week, help us see good everywhere we look. Help us look at the world with a child's eyes. Help us focus on the good things around us over the bad. Thank You, Jesus. Amen.

# Don't Close Your Ears

*Whoever shuts their ears to the cry of the*
*poor will also cry out and not be answered.*

—PROVERBS 21:13

**We have a fairly** loud home. Both of us are extroverts and all four of our kids are as well. We watch sports and play games, often with three or four people talking at the same time. Whether the moment is happy or sad, it is always loud. We love it, but sometimes it gets to be too much. It wouldn't be uncommon late into an evening to see one of us parents hunched over with an index finger in each ear trying to shut the noise out. Sometimes we just don't want to hear it anymore.

Proverbs 21:13 imagines a scenario where someone asking for help receives the same treatment—ears are closed to them. Not in a moderately humorous, loving way, like with our family, but in a brutal way. Maybe you've been in a situation like this, or maybe you've been the one with the opportunity to help. In either case, the implication of the scripture is that if we choose not to help someone when they need it, we may be rejected when we need help.

When we read a verse like this, it's important to remember what Proverbs is and isn't. Proverbs are generally true observations about life. Proverbs are not promises. The writer isn't predicting certain what-goes-around-comes-around energy if we fail to help someone in need. He is simply observing the reality that all people face times of difficulty. In a family, siblings, parents, aunts, uncles, and cousins will all need help at different times for various reasons. If we choose not to help someone in need when we could help them, we may find no one around to help us during our difficult times. So don't stick your fingers in your ears; listen for how God may want you to help.

# Discussion Questions

1. Is there anyone in your family or community who needs help right now?

2. Why do we sometimes not want to help people who need it?

3. What does it feel like to need someone's help and have to ask for it?

4. Do you find it difficult to hear God sometimes? What's one way we can listen for what He is trying to tell us?

## Family Activity

Make a list of all the times in your family's history, big or small, that you had to rely on the goodwill of others. This can include broken-down cars on the side of the road, needing a helping hand after a baby was born, financial issues during a job transition, etc. Then, next to each incident, write down the names of who in your family or community pitched in to help and what they did to support you. Hopefully, you'll notice how memorable and meaningful our sacrificial help can be.

## Action of the Week

When asked for help at school, work, or home, just say yes. For one day or one week, "no" is not allowed. When anyone other than those doing this devotional with you asks you for something, figure out how to say yes.

## Guided Prayer

God, help us this week to see the needs of those who are struggling, and let us always be quick to offer help. Thank You, God, for always helping us. In Jesus's name, Amen.

# The Invitation
# God Gives Us

*Come, all you who are thirsty, come to the
waters; and you who have no money, come,
buy and eat! Come, buy wine and milk
without money and without cost. Why spend
money on what is not bread, and your labor
on what does not satisfy? Listen, listen to me,
and eat what is good, and you will delight in
the richest of fare.*

—ISAIAH 55:1–2

**When our daughter** was three, she wanted to
swim in the pool, but she refused to leave the stairs. On a
family vacation, she convinced us to get in the pool with
her. We wanted her to experience the rest of the pool and
the thrill of jumping in as we caught her! But when we
offered these things, she stubbornly refused; her immense
certainty couldn't be swayed! Although she talks of big
plans to jump off the diving board and swim with her
brothers, we know that as she gets older, she first has to
be willing to get off the steps and take some risks to gain
the totality of what the pool has to offer her.

Isaiah 55 reminds us that God is a giver of good gifts.
He doesn't have a stingy mentality, but one of abundance
and generosity. There are so many blessings that come as
the result of receiving Christ: We receive the Holy Spirit to

lead, guide, and comfort us. We can look forward to eternity in the midst of struggle here on Earth, knowing that God is preparing an amazing place for us. Scripture tells us that God wants to fill us with peace when we share our requests with Him. Through Christ, we have freedom from our past, and we don't have to hold on to it anymore. What lavish riches these are, right? But so often we can be just like the girl in the pool, knowing these things are offered to us but not enjoying them because of fear and doubt of what it would take to gain them. Nothing could be further from the truth. These verses describe our Father's love for us in His invitation to come; there's no RSVP, dress code, or obligation of a gift. He has so much in store for us if we are willing to come and be satisfied by His love and abundant goodness. Forsake any fear that's holding you back and bask in His immense love and benefits toward you.

# Discussion Questions

1. What is something you are holding on to that God wants you to let go of?

2. What risk do you need to take and trust that God will provide?

3. Which benefit of God's goodness, either listed here or elsewhere in the Bible, is one you need to remember this week?

4. So many of God's gifts are free. Can you name some not already mentioned here?

## Family Activity

Throw a party! Spend some time meditating on God's goodness to you this week. Bake a cake, pour sparkling cider in your fanciest cups, and play some music that really makes your heart happy. Rejoice in all God has done for you and in your life, both personally and as a family.

## Action of the Week

Set aside a "kindness bowl" and place little sheets of paper next to it. Each day, write down one small kindness God has shown you this week and place it in the bowl. At the end of the week, read them together to remember His goodness and thank Him for it.

## Guided Prayer

Dear Lord, help us not forget Your goodness to us. Thank You that You offer an open invitation to us without condition and that You want us to enjoy all You have. Help us have hearts of gratitude for who You are and all You have done in our lives. In Jesus's name. Amen.

# They're Rooting for You!

*For everything that was written in the past was written to teach us, so that through the endurance taught in the Scriptures and the encouragement they provide we might have hope.*

—ROMANS 15:4

**When Kristen was** in middle school, she decided she wanted to learn to run cross-country. Her dad took her for a few runs to give her some tips that he adhered to when running. The more she ran, the more she found that the most important tip was to keep running no matter how slow she was going: "Just keep putting one foot in front of the other." These principles were helpful in training, but even more helpful at a race.

At the beginning of a race, the atmosphere encourages you to go as fast as you can and get ahead, whereas if you keep your own pace and have endurance built up, you're more likely to end up passing the people who exerted all their energy at the beginning and have nothing left for the most important part: the end.

Endurance is just as important in life. God's Word is full of stories of people who are ordinary but trust God, and their examples bring us hope to keep going. There are Abraham and Sarah, who trust God for a promise they have to wait twenty-five years for Him to fulfill. There is Noah, who obeys God and builds an ark although he is ridiculed for it (and some interpretations of the Bible say Noah has never even seen rain before). There is Job, who loses just about everything and whose wife tells him to curse God, but he chooses instead to trust God, and he sees everything restored. There is Moses, who is called to lead the Israelites to the promised land though he must endure forty years in the wilderness to get there. There is Ruth, who doesn't give up on her mother-in-law even though there are no benefits to staying by her side, and in her obedience God brings her a new spouse to care for and love her.

The truth is that life is full of opportunities to make you want to give up. But God has graciously given us these examples—as well as the gift of Jesus—to remind us that we can persevere, that there is hope no matter what we are facing. These people don't always get everything right, but they trust God and they are rooting for you to do the same as you believe in Him in the midst of your situation.

# Discussion Questions

1. What areas of your life have you seen God teach you lessons of endurance?

2. What is something that gives you courage to persevere when you feel like giving up? Compare and contrast the encouragement that works for each person in your family.

3. Which of the Bible characters' stories shared here resonates the most with you? Why?

4. This week's verse says that the lessons of endurance and encouragement provided in the scriptures will give us hope. Why is hope so important to our hearts? Why is it so important to our faith?

## Family Activity

Write a note to someone in your family who needs encouragement. Leave it where you know they'll find it. If you'd like to write to someone in your extended family, send it via snail mail. Share a story of when you didn't give up and God blessed you through it. Remind them to have hope and trust in God.

## Action of the Week

Come up with a route to walk or run as a family. Practice encouraging one another through it until the end, no matter how long it takes.

## Guided Prayer

Dear God, we thank You for Your Word, which encourages us not to give up no matter what we face. Thank You for the examples of perseverance of those who have gone before us. Thank You most of all for Jesus, who endured the cross on our behalf so we could have life. Help us live for Him. In Jesus's name, Amen.

# Lighten Up, God Made a Beautiful World

*I know that there is nothing better for people than to be happy and to do good while they live. That each of them may eat and drink, and find satisfaction in all their toil—this is the gift of God.*

—ECCLESIASTES 3:12–13

**Solomon had it all:** money, pleasure, and power beyond what most of us will ever experience. He won wars, collected great wealth, and had great wisdom. He saw the heights of human existence. Yet, in this week's verse, when reflecting on life, he notices the small things—the joy in a project completed, the enjoyment of a good meal, and the simple happiness in doing good. Solomon points us toward our most basic accomplishments: a good meal and a difficult task completed.

In the New Testament, Paul says to Timothy that God "richly provides us with everything for our enjoyment." In the Old Testament, when David describes God's deliverance of Israel in Psalm 126, he says, "Our mouths were filled with laughter, our tongues with songs of joy."

Sometimes followers of Jesus can be a bummer to hang out with because our seriousness about sin and hell can mute our ability to pause and live like today is a good day in this present age. Sometimes families, in our desire to maximize our education, achieve in our sports, and engage in all kinds of activities, are rushing too much to enjoy much of anything.

This scripture points us toward the counterintuitive reality that the most important thing in our enjoyment of life isn't the big stuff, it's our ability to pause and be happy in the small things. God gave us food to eat, a beautiful world, and one another. True followers of Jesus should allow themselves to laugh and eat, and tell stories and eat some more, because while we wait for Jesus to come back, one of the best ways to worship Him is enjoying the things He has made. So let's have no shame in our joy; let's celebrate God's goodness. Everywhere something good is happening, and God is being kind to us.

# Discussion Questions

1. Do you find it easy to take joy in small things?

2. Step outside or look out a window. What are five things you see that show God's goodness to us?

3. What is the most fun your family has had together in the last year?

4. What does the answer to the previous question tell you about priorities for the year ahead?

## Family Activity

Have a family favorites dinner. Let each person make or pick up a favorite dish or treat. Delight in the good food, stopping with each thing you eat to describe what is so good about it. While you eat, have each person tell a favorite story about the family. Try to be super present and joyful, abiding in God's goodness together.

## Action of the Week

Celebrate! This week, no matter how little it seems, do a little dance, sing a little song, or jump up and down every time something good happens. Discipline yourself to see homework completed, teeth well brushed, or the dishes cleaned as something to enjoy. God wants us to.

## Guided Prayer

Dear Lord, help us see the small, good things around us and rejoice in them. Help us see the joy You want us to have and enjoy the life You've given us. Thank You, Jesus. Amen.

# Don't Take the Shortcut

*Ill-gotten treasures have no lasting value, but righteousness delivers from death.*

—PROVERBS 10:2

**Luke's family moved** the summer before he started high school. They enjoyed meeting their new neighbors and exploring the area. One of their neighbors, Mr. X, really loved his lawn. Almost every afternoon and weekend, he worked tirelessly, mowing and trimming and fertilizing.

When school started, Luke remembers realizing that if he walked through Mr. X's backyard into his own backyard and through the back door of his house, he would save about three minutes. The only issue was that after a few days of Luke taking this shortcut, Mr. X called his parents in anger, saying Luke was messing up his grass.

Condition of the grass aside, Luke's experience with Mr. X is what the writer of Proverbs is getting at in our verse for this week. When we try to make things easier or better for ourselves by doing something too fast or making a morally suspect compromise, we inevitably cause long-term damage. Some shortcuts can cause problems even when they work. Whether it's our taxes or physical fitness or a difficult math unit, we must both do the right things and do them in the right way if we want to secure God's blessing.

Notice that the writer of Proverbs doesn't say the shortcut immediately causes disaster. In the metaphor, the "treasures" have been secured. It's just that because they weren't properly earned, they will not bring happiness or fulfillment. Sometimes in life we can get what we want and still end up sorrowful that we did.

# Discussion Questions

1. Is there a tempting shortcut currently available to you?

2. Have you ever "won" a treasure, but later regretted it because of a shortcut you took?

3. Why does the writer of Proverbs see outcomes and process as woven together?

4. What's something you worked for that took you a long time to achieve? How do you think it would have been different if you had cut corners to get the same result?

## Family Activity

Open up a navigation app on a phone or computer. Put in your current address and then a place you often go (church, school, Target, etc.) as a destination. On the map, trace a straight line with your finger from your house to the destination and have a discussion about all the problems that might be caused if you drove in a direct line rather than on the roads provided.

## Action of the Week

No shortcuts. Write on a notecard about any current short-cuts you are tempted to take and recommit yourself to doing things the right way, God's way. Carry the card with you this week as a reminder to do things God's way.

## Guided Prayer

God, help us honor You this week and live well by doing the right thing and avoiding shortcuts. Help us take the path in front of us with courage and grace and keep our eyes fixed on what matters to You. In Jesus's name, Amen.

# Hold Each Other Up

*Carry each other's burdens, and in this way you will fulfill the law of Christ.*

—GALATIANS 6:2

**Every once in a while,** Kristen goes out of town. When she does, she thoughtfully leaves food in the refrigerator and a list of reminders about the kids' activities. No matter how much preparation she does, Luke inevitably finds himself amazed and overwhelmed at how much is needed to keep the household running. To do what she normally does every day, for just a few days, is exhausting.

In this week's verse, Paul speaks about carrying what others carry. When we hold others up, helping them navigate the difficult things they are dealing with, we are loving well. We are also called to carry others *along*. Sometimes a loved one's difficult path is like physically carrying giant barbells around. They can't be removed, but others can help with the weight.

It's often easier to freeze up than to lean in when someone is dealing with something big. Rather than shouldering the weight of a scary diagnosis, frustrating boss, or painful conflict, we give advice. When we talk in a situation that needs action, we usually hurt someone we love. Sometimes, instead of talking, our physical presence or quiet support is a better way to help someone in pain.

"Fulfill the law of Christ" speaks to the example Jesus set for us. He didn't leave us stuck in sin, He saved us from our sin problem. When we engage in understanding, helping with, and staying aware of the struggles our friends and family are in, we are doing the same things Jesus did. In this way, we bless Jesus and our loved ones, too.

# Discussion Questions

1. Is it hard for you to admit you need someone to shoulder the load with you?

2. Have you ever stayed away from someone you know because you weren't sure how to help?

3. Thinking about the cross, how did Jesus bear our burdens?

4. Can you think of a time when you were struggling and someone helped support you?

## Family Activity

As a family, sit on the floor with your legs straight in front of you. One at a time, have each person try to stand up without using their hands. After everyone has tried that, partner up and have someone help you up and see how much easier it is. Talk about the difference between getting up on your own and having the support of a family member.

## Action of the Week

Help, don't talk. For this week, avoid giving advice to your loved ones. Instead, try to figure out what they might need and do what you can to help. This simple turn may surprise you in how much it blesses those around you.

## Guided Prayer

God, help us hold our loved ones up this week by sharing their load. Give us eyes to see others' needs and help us focus on them, not just ourselves. In Jesus's name, Amen.

# How He Does It Is Never the Same

*And my God will meet all your needs according to the riches of His glory in Christ Jesus.*

—PHILIPPIANS 4:19

**With our modern-day,** Westernized worldview, we can read this verse and almost think of God as the genie in *Aladdin*, granting all our wants and wishes. But if that's the way we read the Bible, we've got it all wrong. Paul himself is writing this letter to the church while he is imprisoned for boldly sharing his faith. He's not promising a prosperous, easy life; he's saying, *I have seen God meet my needs and I can confidently proclaim that He will meet yours as well.* The truth is that the Philippian church has been generous and sacrificial in their giving to the church in Jerusalem even amid their own adversity and poverty, and because of that Paul knows God will take care of them.

In 2 Kings 4:1–7, there's a story of a widow who cries out to Elisha begging for help because creditors are coming to take her sons as slaves. He asks her what she has in her house, and she has only one jar of oil. He tells her to borrow vessels from all her neighbors and then go into her house and pour oil into all the vessels she has collected. Asking for vessels and trusting God to fill them must have taken a lot of faith! When she has filled all the vessels, the oil stops flowing. Elisha tells her to use the oil to pay her

85

debts and says that she and her sons can live on the rest. God always provides for our needs (sometimes in miraculous ways). Just like this widow, we can take comfort in the fact that, just as God never lacks glory, we should anticipate no lack in His giving.

# Discussion Questions

1. Do you tend to think of God more like a genie, a generous father, or something else?

2. Is it difficult for you to give to others? In which area do you think it's hardest for you to give: your time, your money, or your talents and abilities?

3. Have you ever given something to someone even if you felt you didn't have enough for yourself? What happened? If not, what is a way you can give to someone sacrificially?

4. What sticks out to you the most about the story of the widow?

## Family Activity

God gives us gifts so we can bless others with them. Have everyone in the family take a spiritual giftings test to see specific areas in which God has gifted you. You might find that you have a gift of leadership, service, teaching, mercy, or any number of others. Read through the results. Do they surprise you? Find a way to serve your family, friends, or church using one of your giftings this week. You can find spiritual gift tests at GiftsTest.com.

## Action of the Week

Memorize Luke 6:38 this week, which says, "Give, and it will be given to you. A good measure, pressed down, shaken together and running over, will be poured into your lap. For with the measure you use, it will be measured to you."

## Guided Prayer

Dear God, thank You for being so good to us that You supply every specific need we have. We pray for patience, faith, and obedience as we wait for the provision we need, in Your time and in Your way. In Jesus's name, Amen.

# Joy Is the Overflow

*You make known to me the path of life; you
will fill me with joy in your presence, with
eternal pleasures at your right hand.*

—PSALM 16:11

**The summer after** we graduated high school,
we went on a mission trip to Guatemala. We spent the
majority of our time building a brick road in a community.
Throughout the week, we got to know the people there,
and despite the language barrier we felt a growing bond.
The people in the community didn't have many material
belongings but their joy in knowing Jesus was immense.
Their joy in knowing and seeing God's provision in their
lives for everything that they needed was inspiring, as was
their desire to encourage us in the bond we have as brothers and sisters in Christ.

Many people say they want joy, but they find it elusive
because true joy is found in God's presence. Joy isn't a quick
solution or something you can buy online. Galatians 5:22
says that joy is a fruit of the Spirit because it comes out of
our relationship with God. It's found in trusting God to show
us the path ahead and letting ourselves be guided by His
Spirit. It's not mustered through sheer will or determination
on our part but through our relationship with Him, His Word,
and those who love Him.

There's an acronym that says joy stands for "Jesus,
others, yourself." When we are abiding in God and depending on Him for everything, our focus is less on ourselves

and more on God and others. Material things might fulfill us temporarily, but they will inevitably wear out or break, or we may lose interest after a while. God's joy, however, is lasting. Joy trusts that God is at work even if you can't see it, because you know your hope is found in God alone.

# Discussion Questions

1. Have you ever seen joy displayed that was so attractive to you that you wanted to replicate it in your life? What do you think is the difference between happiness and joy?

2. How does focusing on yourself prevent joy?

3. How can you spend more time this week with God or His people in a way that brings you joy?

4. Have you ever felt joy even when you were lacking something? What was it? Share with your family.

## Family Activity

Whatever is inside someone will eventually come out! This week, demonstrate this point with a baking soda volcano experiment. You will need baking soda, a small cup, red food coloring, a squeeze bottle, vinegar, dish soap, a spoon, and a tray. In a bowl, mix together ¼ cup of baking soda, a drop of food coloring, and a tablespoon of water. Add a drop of dish soap on top. Fill the squeeze bottle with equal parts water and vinegar. Start spraying the squeeze bottle mixture into the bowl and watch the eruption. Imagine God's presence filling you with joy and that joy overflowing to your family and your community.

## Action of the Week

This week, set a goal to encourage the family members that you see displaying joy even when their circumstances aren't favorable. Support them when they feel frustrated, and let them know that you are trusting God with them to work in their situation.

## Guided Prayer

Dear God, thank You for the joy that comes from spending time in Your Word and with Your people. Thank You for the joy You give when we are trusting You in the midst of difficulty. We pray for joy to overflow from our hearts. In Jesus's name, Amen.

# Pick Each Other Up

*Brothers and sisters, if someone is caught in a sin, you who live by the Spirit should restore that person gently.*

—GALATIANS 6:1

**Our least favorite time** of day is the fifteen minutes before the kids go to bed. We enjoy chatting during teeth brushing, and the endless requests for more water don't even bother us. What drives us crazy is the collaborative effort to clean up the toys. To try and keep things fair and be supportive of one another, our family always cleans up together, not passing off the task to the person who made the mess. Bending down over and over to grab the little cars and blocks is not fun at all.

Picking toys up is not much fun, but picking up people can be even less so. When people get "caught in a sin," we are usually so frustrated with them that the last thing we want to do is help. Whether it's a big, onetime mess-up or a long-term habit of failure, Paul calls us in Galatians 6 to gently and mercifully pick up people who fall.

Our typical impulse is to punish, explode at, or withdraw from the person who made a mistake, hoping to make them feel the same pain we do. This may feel good for a moment, but it does not produce any improvement or change. Hurting someone because they hurt you does nothing to help.

We must be gentle. That's the word the Bible uses to describe the process of picking someone up. Not brutal, aggressive, or strong. When we fall down, we can be so blinded and confused that only when someone is patient toward us can we see how to return to a good path.

If we want our family to be a healthy place to grow, we must pick each other up when we fall. That means more grace, more patience, and more picking up the little Lego pieces even after we step on them for the hundredth time.

# Discussion Questions

1. How does your family handle cleaning up messes? Do you clean all together or individually? How are chores divided in your house?

2. Why is it so tempting to kick people who are down rather than pick them up?

3. Have you ever had someone be kind to you after a big failure? What did it feel like? How did it help?

4. How should we talk to someone who is feeling down after a big mistake?

## Family Activity

Have a pick-up contest. Take three board games out, preferably ones with smaller pieces of some kind. Dump each of them out on the floor in a big pile. Using a timer or a stopwatch, measure how long it takes the family to pick them up and put them away flawlessly. See how fast you can do it as a team, without picking sides or forcing the work on someone else. Play a second round and see if you can improve your time.

## Action of the Week

This week, as a reminder to pick people up who fall down, try to pick up anything you see out of place—garbage on the street, clothes on the floor, a poster in the hallway at school, anything. Let this action remind your heart to do the same for others.

## Guided Prayer

Dear Lord, help us pick up others who are down this week. Give us a spirit of gentleness toward those who are struggling. In Jesus's name, Amen.

# We See Ourselves as Really Good

*A person may think their own ways are right,
but the Lord weighs the heart.*

—PROVERBS 21:2

**Almost always,** when a police officer pulls someone over, the first question they ask is "Do you know why I stopped you?" Sometimes it's clear; other times it's not. The point of the question seems obvious to us: When you can get someone to admit their own mistake, the process of dealing with it is much easier.

Our family fights sometimes. We have disagreements about gaming controllers and dishwasher unloading and where to go for dinner. These can be comical fights and they can also be hurtful, but at the core of almost every fight is a difference of perspective. One person sees themselves as correct and the other person as wrong.

We tend to see ourselves as pretty virtuous. Even when we hurt others or make mistakes, we see our choices as motivated by something good. We use our internal sense of a proper motive to tell ourselves we are all good. So, when someone tries to tell us we failed or hurt them, we usually retreat to an explanation of why it isn't that big of a deal or we didn't mean to or it isn't our fault.

Our verse for today teaches that God ultimately knows the truth about what is in our hearts. He knows the reality of what is "fair" and what is kind. Sometimes our desire to get our way and prove our points in family relationships can get in the way of our calling to love. When we need to be right, it is very hard for us to love. Our perspective is limited, and other perspectives can certainly be helpful, but only God sees all.

# Discussion Questions

1. Does your family have any ongoing disagreements that reveal different perspectives?

2. Can you think of a time when a family member's explanation changed your perspective?

3. How can the fact that God sees the whole picture bring comfort?

4. Instead of getting defensive or making excuses, what's one thing we can do or say when someone tells us we've hurt them?

## Family Activity

How do we see one another? Play a version of the game Illustrations. Give each member of the family a piece of paper and a pen. Each person should draw a picture of someone in the family without saying who they're drawing. Then have them pass the paper to another person and make them guess who it is. The inevitable confusion illustrates how our own perspectives—and our ability to communicate—can be limited.

## Action of the Week

Try using the phrase "from my perspective" when having conflict conversations this week. It's a gentle way of reminding yourself and the person you are talking to of the limits of personal perspective.

## Guided Prayer

God, this week we ask You to help us see our own perspectives as limited, others' perspectives as helpful, and Yours as perfect. Help us not assume that we know better, but to try to see others' perspectives. In Jesus's name, Amen.

# Only God Gives the Growth

*I planted the seed, Apollos watered it, but God has been making it grow. So neither the one who plants nor the one who waters is anything, but only God who makes things grow. The one who plants and the one who waters have one purpose, and they will each be rewarded according to their own labor.*

—1 CORINTHIANS 3:6–8

**It's pretty cool** that we as Christians have an opportunity to "water" and "plant" things for the kingdom. But this scripture doesn't mess around about who the glory should go to; it says twice in two verses that *God gives the growth*. Interestingly, these verses follow a confrontation over a "who taught whom" argument going on in the church. At this point in the chapter, Paul is saying, "Okay, okay, let's stop dropping names!" The glory isn't going to any of us. Paul wants the church to remember that as Christians we can have a role in the kingdom, and God wants us to use our gifts to serve Him with all our heart. But God is, and will always be, the fertilizer that makes the ministry grow.

Before COVID-19 hit in 2020, Kristen had planned to start a women's ministry small group and she nearly backed out of it once everything shut down. To be honest, it seemed like that would have been easier. But during that time of isolation, the group went forward, and the seeds and work of planting and watering ended up bringing encouragement that was imperative—and not just for Kristen; the group grew as friends told friends about it. Had she chosen not to obey, she wouldn't have been able to experience the joy of seeing Him bring the fruit from seeds planted. Some of the women in the group lived alone and had lost people because of the pandemic; this group brought community at a moment when that was hard to come by. As the group members discussed what they were learning from the meetings, they shared what they were learning in other circles as well, and what could have been a stagnant spiritual time in their lives became a moment to flourish.

We may also experience seasons where God grows things in us instead of around us. Like a landscape overhaul, there are times when soul work like forgiveness or grief are necessary. Those moments don't always reveal fruit you can see, but they always bring health that is crucial for well-being and wholeness for you and those around you. Although it is often hard-fought and sometimes even unseen, we know God will give the growth in His appointed time.

# Discussion Questions

1. Is there an area of your life where God has brought growth in the last few months or the past year?

2. Is there a situation you feel God is calling you to water, whether it's in your own life or someone else's? What is a seed you've planted in someone's life?

3. Imagine one of your family members is feeling discouraged because something they want to grow is

taking a long time. What could you say to encourage them?

4. What about this Bible verse or commentary resonates with your life and why?

## Family Activity

Grow an indoor or outdoor plant (depending on the climate) and have each family member help feed and water it. Keep it somewhere prominent in your home. You can even give it a name. Use it as a reminder that God gives the growth. Share with each other what areas He's grown in you since planting it.

## Action of the Week

Write a list of how each person in the family is trying to grow emotionally, relationally, and spiritually. Pray specifically and fervently that God will give the growth.

## Guided Prayer

Dear God, we thank You for allowing us to work for Your kingdom. Help us know where to plant and water, and not to give up even when we don't see growth. Please bring growth in us and in the work of our hands. In Jesus's name, Amen.

# Resentment Makes Misery

---

*But they saw him in the distance, and before he reached them, they plotted to kill him. "Here comes that dreamer!" they said to each other.*

—GENESIS 37:18–19

---

**Luke, admittedly, has never been** able to dunk a basketball. His average height and limited vertical leap got in the way. In all his years of playing basketball, he always felt a little jealous of the guys who could get up and slam the ball with fury. But just because he could not do what they could do, would it have been okay for him to despise them?

In Genesis, Joseph has a vivid dream that his brothers will one day work for him. In his youthful exuberance, he tells them all about it. It makes them so mad that after they stew on it for a while, they decide they want to kill him. This is not rational or reasonable behavior, but it is what sometimes happens when we get bitter.

People hurt us. People frustrate us by having more than we have. They say and do things that cause pain. But when we reduce another human being to nothing more or less than the thing they did that hurt us, we are losing. Especially when it comes to family. Family needs to be the place of highest support and lowest comparison. Having a healthy family means being happy for one another, even if we sometimes wish the situation were different.

When Joseph's brothers allow themselves to become bitter, they try to kill him. This choice is something they deeply regret decades later. The same will be true for you. If you let yourself become resentful or jealous of those you love, it will cause harm down the road. God may not give you the exact skills or achievements you desire, but He will be good to you, and the gifts He does give you are special and part of His perfect plan for your life. The only way you can ruin it is by choosing misery over joy.

# Discussion Questions

1. Does anyone in the family have a gift or skill you wish you had?

2. Have you ever found it hard not to be jealous of someone close to you? Why is it so hard not to become jealous of people we love?

3. Have you ever gotten rid of jealousy? How did you do it?

4. We all have our own special gifts given by God. What is a gift or skill of yours that someone else might wish they had?

## Family Activity

Compliment yourself. Go around the table, and each of you say something positive about yourself. Rather than praising others and feeling a little bad, feel good about the ways God has made you instead. If you struggle at all, ask your family for help in naming things that are wonderful about you. Psalm 139 says each of us is "wonderfully made." Celebrate that in yourself.

## Action of the Week

Remember what you have. Every time you see a possession or talent that you wish you had, immediately speak out loud (quietly or in your mind, if you're in public) what you do have from God. If needed, keep the thought in your heart to remind you. Focusing on what you have is the best antidote to feeling bitter about what someone else has.

## Guided Prayer

Dear Lord, help us see the people we love, not the things they do that bother us. Help us, Lord, to trust You, not our own sense of what should happen. In Jesus's name, Amen.

# We Are Known by What We Do

---

*Do not lie to each other, since you have taken off your old self with its practices and have put on the new self, which is being renewed in knowledge in the image of its Creator.*

—COLOSSIANS 3:9–10

---

**Which NBA basketball player** used to stick out his tongue as he made a shot? Who waves their hand with their fingers together as they stand on a balcony? Odds are, many of you know the answers to these questions. Little boys and girls have often imitated both people. Many kids dream of being a queen or a princess or an all-star on the court, and as they've seen these visuals, they've imitated what they want to be when they grow up.

God wants us to imitate Him in the same way. In Him, there are no lies—He cannot lie because He is truth, and He expects us to model that. When we accept Jesus into our hearts, He makes us a new creation. We won't have new bodies until Heaven, but here on Earth our hearts are transformed to be more like Him, to act like He does, and to have words that reflect Him. We bring Him glory when we represent Him well.

In Genesis, we see the serpent lie to Eve in the garden, and because she listens and is deceived, we all deal with sin. One lie has big repercussions—our sin always finds us out. It doesn't matter if we think it's only a little untruth,

God always brings things to light. Just like Michael Jordan is known for sticking his tongue out while making a shot and the queen of England is known by her wave, we are known by what we do whether someone is watching or not. How do you want to represent God?

# Discussion Questions

1. Has someone ever lied to you? How did it make you feel?

2. Have you ever been caught in a lie that was found out? What happened? What area of your life do you find it most difficult to have integrity in?

3. How have you seen God transform you since you accepted Jesus into your heart?

4. What do you want to be when you grow up (or what did you want to be when you were younger)? What quality or characteristic would you like to be known for?

## Family Activity

Play "Three Truths and a Lie." Have each person say four things about themselves. Three of these should be true things, and one should be a lie. Have everyone playing try to figure out which one the lie is. Talk about how easy it is to twist the truth and how we have to be discerning about the truth. Also, discuss integrity and how it is important to always tell the truth because of how people perceive you if they feel they can't trust what you say.

## Action of the Week

Memorize 2 Corinthians 8:21, which says, "For we are taking pains to do what is right, not only in the eyes of the Lord but also in the eyes of man." Use this verse as a reminder to do what's right whether anyone can see you or not!

## Guided Prayer

Dear God, thank You for Your Word and that we can always look to You for the truth. Thank You that Your truth puts our hearts on the right path. Help us represent You well with integrity in every area of our lives. In Jesus's name, Amen.

# If You Are Looking, You Can Always Find a Reason

*The sluggard says, "There's a lion outside! I'll be killed in the public square!"*

—PROVERBS 22:13

In his book *Great by Choice*, business author Jim Collins talks about the idea of "productive paranoia." It's the idea that wise business leaders over-forecast potential problems so they aren't caught unprepared and unable to respond. They over-concentrate on things that could potentially destroy their mission. This is a good thing, as long as it doesn't go too far.

Often in families, a parent takes on the role of making sure everyone is safe and that details are attended to so no one gets hurt. Reasonable safety is important. Just because we have faith doesn't mean we avoid seat belts or home insurance. But concerns about safety can occasionally morph over time into a desire for control or a refusal to live life to the fullest.

Some people use concern for safety as an excuse to avoid trying anything. If you are looking for one, there is always a reason not to do something. Our minds are capable of finding endless excuses.

In the book of Proverbs, if the sluggard is saying something, it's wrong. The sluggard loves self and ignores God.

Everything he does, says, and thinks is wrong. The sluggard is lazy and looks for any excuse to do nothing. The irony is that there is no lion outside. The sluggard imagines problems that don't exist to avoid having to do what he should. The sluggard isn't reasonably considering safety, he's trying to avoid trying anything at all.

We don't want to be the sluggard; we want to be wise.

Did you struggle at a sport you really wanted to do well in? Did someone you trusted hurt you? Have you suffered a setback that makes it easy to give up?

Not wanting to lean out and risk yourself is totally understandable, but we must. When we start imagining problems that aren't really problems to avoid trying again, we are not only hurting ourselves, but also hurting the family we love.

# Discussion Questions

1. Do you consider yourself more safety conscious or a risk taker?

2. Have you ever found reasons not to do something out of fear?

3. How do we know if challenges or cautions are real or imagined? How do we discern the truth of a situation?

4. Can you think of a time when you were afraid to try something, but you did it anyway? What was the outcome?

## Family Activity

Go around the table naming zoo animals. As soon as one is named, everyone else at the table should immediately say "scary" or "not scary" based on whether you would feel okay if you saw one in the street. Keep a list and playfully argue about which animals would actually be scary if seen in person, and why.

## Action of the Week

Try to eliminate unreasonable fear by labeling it. Whether you're in heavy traffic, giving a presentation at work, learning a tricky play at a sports practice, or talking to a new person, try to say to yourself every time you start feeling nervous, "I don't have to be scared of this." The purpose isn't to pretend fear isn't real, but to try to take some possession over the things that bother us.

## Guided Prayer

Dear Lord, help us be wise, using our days and time wisely to serve You well. Help us trust You even when we're unsure rather than running from fears, real or imagined. Thank You, Jesus. Amen.

# Choose the Right Tool

*And we urge you, brothers and sisters, warn those who are idle and disruptive, encourage the disheartened, help the weak, be patient with everyone.*

—1 THESSALONIANS 5:14

**Not much is more frustrating** for a young family than a drive home with a young child screaming. In our family, Luke tends to view this problem as something willful (the child is rebellious and needs to be corrected). Kristen tends to view this problem as something systematic (the baby was kept out too late and is overtired). Each of us views and solves problems differently. Both of us have made mistakes in parenting by assuming we knew what one of our children needed.

There's an old saying, attributed to Abraham Maslow, that goes, "If the only tool you have is a hammer, [you] treat everything as if it were a nail." Different problems require different strategies to solve. Someone refusing to do something should be handled much differently from someone who doesn't know how. We cause tension and hurt in our families when we try to deal with every situation the same way.

Rather than starting with the "what" of a problem, we do better if we start with a "why." A baby can be crying because something hurts, because they are hungry, or because they are tired. The same can be true for an irri-table grandparent or a frustrated teenager. We can't help each other until we understand why someone is acting the way they are.

Paul is telling us to look at the situation. Does the person need to be challenged? Do they need encour-agement? Do they need comfort? This is true for parents reacting to children, but also for children dealing with parents. When we see a situation clearly, it becomes much easier to help and not hurt with our words.

# Discussion Questions

1. Do you find it easiest to see others as ignorant (they don't know how to do something), discouraged (something must be upsetting them), or hardheaded (they're being selfish)?

2. When you are frustrated or upset, what reaction from the family helps you the most?

3. Can you think of a time when you misunderstood someone and hurt them without meaning to?

4. Look up the meaning of "disheartened." What's one way we can "encourage the disheartened," as Paul says in this week's verse?

## Family Activity

Role-play how to examine a situation. Make three note cards for each person in your family. One should say "warn," one should say "encourage," and one should say "help." Now create a hypothetical scenario, as in "Mom got a flat tire on the way home and she's late making dinner," or "Micah forgot to study for a math quiz and received a poor grade." Discuss as a family which response will most likely help the person move forward in a positive way.

## Action of the Week

Try to ask "why" in a positive way as much as possible. Every time you get frustrated, use a sincere, honest, and gentle tone. Ask the person (being very careful not to sound annoyed or angry), "Can you help me understand why you did that?" By starting with curiosity, we are much more likely to have positive outcomes relationally.

## Guided Prayer

God, help us think before we speak this week, trying to understand each other more than fix each other. Help us always think the best of each other, knowing when to warn, when to encourage, and when to help. In Jesus's name, Amen.

# Eyes to See

*In everything I did, I showed you that by this kind of hard work we must help the weak, remembering the words the Lord Jesus himself said: "It is more blessed to give than to receive."*

—ACTS 20:35

**Every Christmas,** we take the kids to a discount store chain to shop for gifts for the family. Luke sits at a nearby coffee shop with the other kids while Kristen shops with them individually. This year, we were struck by the generosity of one of our sons. He came in with his own money, which he had earned and saved, and as he shopped, he delightedly searched to find the most perfect item for each person. Before going to the register, he totaled his items and realized he would spend all he had. He could have easily spent less and kept some money for himself, but he found joy in knowing that each person's reaction would make his sacrifice as the giver worth it.

This scripture reminds us that we have a responsibility as believers to help those who need it. Often there are opportunities all around us, but we close our eyes to them or we're not willing to extend what we have to others. Admittedly, giving can be a struggle, especially when your own needs are substantial. True generosity comes out of a heart that says, "I'm giving by faith and believe that God will make up the difference."

There are lots of ways to give. God has gifted each of us with gifts to use for Him twenty-four hours a day. Jesus gave to all people whether they could give back or not, and when we follow His example, His very image is displayed in us—whether it's Christmastime or not.

# Discussion Questions

1. Who is someone in your life who could use your help? What do they need and what can you give them?

2. Can you recall a time that you were feeling weak and God provided a person or a provision that was an encouragement to you?

3. What are ways you could give to others through your money, your time, and the gifts that God has given you?

4. Think about a gift you gave someone that was wonderfully well received. What was it and how did you feel when you gave it?

## Family Activity

As a family, look up verses together about God's strength and how He helps us in our weakness. Make a list or post one or two on the refrigerator that particularly inspire you. Then write a note to a friend, neighbor, or loved one who is struggling and could use encouragement.

## Action of the Week

As a family, make a meal for someone in your life who could use encouragement. This could be someone who's ill or injured, an older neighbor who doesn't cook for themselves much anymore, or a relative caring for a newborn. Feeding someone is a wonderful way to show love, and it doesn't have to cost a fortune. Show your generosity through a meal.

## Guided Prayer

Dear God, thank You for helping us in our weakness. Thank You for the time, finances, and gifts that You have given us to serve others. Help us be Your hands and feet this week, and help us have eyes to see those You have put in our path to help. Help us become more like You. In Jesus's name, Amen.

# Staying Out of the Headlines

*[Martha] came to him and asked, "Lord, don't you care that my sister has left me to do the work by myself? Tell her to help me!" "Martha, Martha," the Lord answered, "you are worried and upset about many things, but few things are needed—or indeed only one. Mary has chosen what is better, and it will not be taken away from her."*

—LUKE 10:38–42

**Since the beginning of time,** siblings have had a way of pointing out what their brother or sister is doing wrong. Often they divulge the details of something done behind closed doors at opportune moments to make themselves look just a little bit better.

Mary in this particular story gets it right, but Martha is so frustrated and insistent that Jesus see what she is doing that she points out to Him what Mary *isn't* doing. Normally, you'd think Jesus would be the place to go if you're looking for some empathy. But in this situation, Jesus reminds Martha of what's more important. This story reveals that even in the presence of Jesus, our humanness desires to be right and point out our sibling's wrongdoing.

In our home, we've found that our kids go through seasons where they're "in the headlines" more than other times—so much so that we've coined the phrase "out of the headlines." This means that if your sibling (sometimes more than one!) is struggling on a given day and experiencing discipline or just can't seem to get things right, it's in your best interests not to chime in and share all the other reasons why they are "naughty." Instead, we ask our kids to be grateful for the blessing of being on the right track that day. We find this phrase helpful because it's a reminder of how it feels to be on the other side of all the attention.

Because we know the Bible is relevant for our lives today, we know that these stories were written for our instruction. Jesus didn't use perfect people; He used people who were willing to listen to Him and follow Him. If it's been a week where you're feeling more like Martha, know that Jesus doesn't want that to come between you and your sibling. He wants you both to follow what's right.

# Discussion Questions

1. We likely all have days when we feel more like Mary and days when we feel more like Martha. How do you relate to each one?

2. When do you find yourself most "in the headlines"? Is there a situation or behavior you can adjust to help you be in the headlines less?

3. Do you struggle with comparison with your siblings? How can that be helpful and how can that be a hindrance?

4. Jesus tells Martha to focus on Him because He loves her, as He loves all of us, and doesn't want her to be separated from Him. How can this help us when we feel like we're not getting anything right?

## Family Activity

In this story, Jesus reveals that the most important thing is to put Him as priority in your life. Sometimes that is difficult with all the activities that fill up our schedules. Plot out a time for your family to go on a hike or a walk where you can talk, listen to God, and see the beauty that He has made. If there's a moment where a family member is struggling, encourage them along.

## Action of the Week

When the siblings in your family are "in the headlines" this week, instead of chiming in about what they have done wrong, take a moment to silently pray for them, that their hearts will change in the way that's needed.

## Guided Prayer

Dear God, thank You for the siblings You have placed in our lives. Thank You for these God-given relationships, even when those relationships are difficult. Lord, please give patience, grace, and encouragement to everyone in our family. We pray in the name of Jesus. Amen.

# Never Say Never

*So the other disciples told him, "We have seen the Lord!" But he said to them, "Unless I see the nail marks in his hands and put my finger where the nails were, and put my hand into his side, I will not believe."*

—JOHN 20:25

**Jesus's disciple "doubting Thomas"** gets his nickname right after Jesus's resurrection. Although Thomas is not with the disciples, Jesus appears to them, proving to them that he is, in fact, alive again. He shows them the wounds in his hands and his side as proof. We aren't told where Thomas is, but we know he has just lost his dear friend in a really brutal way, and his emotions are probably quite real and raw. It likely causes even more emotional turmoil when the disciples tell him they have seen the Lord.

Eight days later, Thomas is with the disciples when Jesus appears to them. He tells Thomas to put his hands in His wounds, saying, "Stop doubting and believe." You can imagine Thomas's response: "My Lord and my God!" Even in his doubt, Thomas is met with compassion, grace, and a truth he can literally touch. Jesus doesn't belittle him, He personally fills in the gap of Thomas's questions, and in the midst of their relationship He in effect says, I see you, I love you, and I want you to know the truth.

When we get down to it, this story reveals that God loves each person even when they have big doubts. He wants you to bring those things to Him so He can show you that even in the wondering there is meaning and purpose. His power reigns even over the things you don't understand yet.

# Discussion Questions

1. Have you ever had an experience where you were sure something would never happen and then it did?

2. Do you feel like you can bring your doubts to God or your close friends and family? Why or why not?

3. What doubts are you specifically struggling with right now?

4. It's easy to doubt, especially when you want so badly to believe something and you don't want to be disappointed. What are some ways we know that God's promises to us are real?

## Family Activity

Make bracelets together. Get out some letter beads and string and create bracelets that say "trust" or "believe." Wear your bracelets if you'd like, or keep them on your dresser to serve as visual reminders when you are struggling with doubt. They can help you as you face messy situations that you don't completely understand. You can also make a few extra and give them out. Use them to encourage others you know who are facing doubt.

## Action of the Week

Give each family member a piece of paper they can use during the week to write their doubts. Every night before you go to bed, pray together that God will bring peace or answers for the doubts that each person is struggling with. See what God does!

Dear God, thank You for meeting us in our doubt. Thank You that You treat us the same way You treated Thomas, with compassion, grace, and truth. Please help us bring our doubts to You and reveal to us what we need to know to walk in peace and truth. In Jesus's name, Amen.

# Keep Your Heart Safe

*Above all else, guard your heart, for
everything you do flows from it.*

—PROVERBS 4:23

**Do you remember** the beginning of the
COVID-19 pandemic? In March 2020, no one really knew
what was happening yet. Before all the politics and argu-
ing, there was simply a desire to keep ourselves safe
from what we didn't yet understand. People were taking
what seemed like extreme measures: scrubbing grocery
packages, hoarding toilet paper, picking up food without
interacting with anyone, anything they could think of to try
not to get infected.

Proverbs 4:23 talks about this kind of vigilance, only
rather than keeping our bodies from disease, the writer of
Proverbs wants us to keep our hearts safe from foolish-
ness. Your heart is the center of you. It's where body, mind,
emotions, and will come together. Everything you do starts
in your heart, so it must be kept clean and clear so your
words and choices are clean as well.

Sometimes we find ourselves doing negative or
unhealthy things without really understanding why. One of
the reasons is that our actions overflow from what's happening in our hearts. We must make sure we don't allow
anything bad into our hearts, so that bad things don't
come out.

As we experience life, we learn what we can and can't
handle, what is and isn't good for us. These lessons can be

somewhat trivial, like knowing your body doesn't react well to spicy food at night or that scary movies really mess with your sleep. They can also be tremendously serious: noticing that a song that reminds you of a bad breakup can send you spiraling emotionally or that looking at an old friend's social media account makes you jealous. To guard or keep your heart is to pay attention to what blesses and grieves you, making sure you give your emotions a healthy diet.

# Discussion Questions

1. What is something that hurts your heart that might surprise people who know you?

2. Think of a time when you did or said something that wasn't really "you." What do you think caused you to do it? What might have prevented it?

3. What kind of habits help us guard our hearts?

4. Why does what we put into our hearts have such an impact on what comes out of them?

## *Family Activity*

Get three glasses and some chocolate syrup. Fill one glass with water, one with milk, and one with soda. Slowly put a little bit of the syrup into each liquid, noticing how long it takes for the color to change. What does each glass full of liquid look like now? Discuss how each of our hearts is different—like the liquids, we react or respond differently to the same stimulus.

## Action of the Week

Try to notice your reactions and share them. When a song or YouTube video or advertisement bothers you, tell your family, asking for insight on why. We all have experiences that play into who we are, and noticing and telling others about them helps us protect one another.

## Guided Prayer

God, help us notice this week what hurts us and avoid it the best we can. Protect our hearts and help us keep them clean and clear. Thank You, Jesus. Amen.

# Should You Do Good Even If You Don't See the Result?

*Let us not become weary in doing good, for at the proper time we will reap a harvest if we do not give up. Therefore, as we have opportunity, let us do good to all people, especially to those who belong to the family of believers.*

—GALATIANS 6:9–10

**Suburban Chicago in the fall** is one of our favorite seasons. The mornings turn crisp, the leaves change, and the temperatures are mild. The shift in season signals that the farmers are in the process of gathering their crops. The corn stalks one day can block your view and be gone the next—you know it's been a good growing year if the corn is "knee high by July." But whether the corn is high or not, harvest time is when the rubber meets the road. The farmers have planted, tended to the crops, and been conscientious about the elements, hoping that surprising weather doesn't strike and ruin all the crops. No hours are too long during harvest time. Farmers want to get their crops before something could potentially destroy them. Let's face it—by the end of the harvest they are exhausted. They know a break is coming, but they have to endure until the job is done, ensuring a bountiful reaping—enough crop for their family and to sell for profit.

Sometimes a farmer can work diligently, with great fervor, and still not see the results they hope for. The same can be true in our jobs, our musical or artistic endeavors, or playing sports. We can experience this outcome when we're struggling to pay off debt or fix a difficult relationship. We live in an era of immediate gratification and satisfaction, and often when we do good but don't see immediate results, we wonder if it really *was* good. We must remember to do what God instructs us in His Word, which is to do good, period. In Galatians, Paul is encouraging us to be patient. While we wait on the payoff, he wants us not to miss out on opportunities but to take action and bless others, both outside the church and within it.

# Discussion Questions:

1. What do you think is the "harvest" Paul is talking about here? What payoff is he envisioning?

2. What makes you weary in doing good? When do you feel like giving up?

3. Was there a time you patiently waited for a payoff after doing good and you found the patience worthwhile?

4. What are some opportunities you could pursue to help believers in your life who could use your encouragement?

## Family Activity

Try to encourage each person in your family this week with this verse when they are weary. If possible, memorize the verse as a way to encourage one another to not give up. When trying to memorize a verse, it is usually helpful to post it in places you see often, like the refrigerator or the bathroom sink.

## Action of the Week

Find a way to serve at your church as a family, whether in the children's ministry, through an administrative task, or even by greeting people before services. Have a conversation afterward to discuss how it was beneficial to other believers and how it may have been wearying for you.

## Guided Prayer

Dear God, thank You for the opportunities You have put in our lives to do good. We pray that You would give us strength to wait on You with patience. Help us not grow weary but continue in Your work knowing that our work for You is not in vain. In Jesus's name, Amen.

# All In for God

*But if serving the Lord seems undesirable
to you, then choose for yourselves this day
whom you will serve, whether the gods your
ancestors served beyond the Euphrates, or
the gods of the Amorites, in whose land you
are living. But as for me and my household,
we will serve the Lord.*

—JOSHUA 24:15

**When Kristen was a freshman** in high school,
she made the competitive cheerleading team that placed
ninth in the state. If she wasn't busy with school or cheerleading, friends and family consumed her time. But as she
filled her schedule, there wasn't a sense of joy; instead, her
busy days had the opposite effect. She was on the hunt
for something that would fill her with true joy. The summer
after her freshman year, a few of her friends invited her on
a mission trip to Oklahoma. On that trip, a pastor preached
the message that only God could fill that void in her
life; cheerleading wouldn't do it, relationships would fall
short, even family, which was such a great asset in her life,
wouldn't ever fulfill her completely.

Ecclesiastes 3:11 says that God has "set eternity in the
human heart." Our hearts will only be satisfied through
knowing Jesus, living for Him, and serving Him. In the
Bible, Joshua is called to lead the Israelite people after
Moses has passed on. He leads the Israelites a long way

before coming to the fork in the road that many of us encounter: Will we serve our wants and desires, or will we serve the Lord? So often life distracts us with desirable things that become like gods in our lives—sports, school, music, popularity, prosperity, and even family togetherness. Many of these things can be good, but when we idolize them above everything else, we run the risk of worshipping them rather than the one true God.

# Discussion Questions

1. Have you ever felt like something in your life was becoming more important than your relationship with God?

2. What is something you do to find fulfillment and joy? Has there been something in your life that you thought would fulfill you and didn't?

3. If someone else was looking at your life, do you think they would say that you are living "all in" for God?

4. What are some things someone might observe about your life that show you serving God rather than yourself?

## Family Activity

Make a family plaque that includes some or all of Joshua 24:15 on it. Have everyone in the family add some flair and their name to it, and post it by your front door where you can see it each time you leave the house. Let it be a reminder of Whom you are serving as you go out to your job, school, and community. Use it to keep you

focused on God amid all the facets of your life and everything the world offers.

## Action of the Week

Write out the activities your family has this week. Allow
it to be a survey of how your family is using its time and
what you are serving, both individually and as a group. Use
this as a guide to look at different areas of your lives and
make adjustments that align with your values.

## Guided Prayer

Thank You, God, for the opportunity to serve You in all
things. Help us fix our eyes on You at all times. Guard us
against distractions that can fill up our lives. Lord, help our
home be a beacon of light for You. In Jesus's name, Amen.

# Catch the Foxes

*For if you forgive other people when they sin against you, your heavenly Father will also forgive you. But if you do not forgive others their sins, your Father will not forgive your sins.*

—MATTHEW 6:14–15

**Foxes are known for being** sly predators looking for their next meal. They'll often raid anywhere they can find food. Even though they seem cute, they are sneaky and willing to injure to get what they want, and their aggressive behavior can quickly change their surroundings. In Song of Songs 2:15, the writer cautions that "the little foxes" will "ruin the vineyards" if we aren't careful.

Unforgiveness is often like a sly fox. It prances into our lives, and before we realize it, it's ravaged our hearts and relationships as well as our relationships with God. Unforgiveness is often like putting on a pair of glasses that makes you see everything through a lens of frustration and hurt, leaving you with an unwillingness to let go of what happened.

But when we remember the sinful and desperate state we were in before we came into relationship with Jesus and what He forgave us for, we can stand to be merciful to others. In that moment, we can take the glasses off and choose forgiveness ourselves. The truth is, like most things, forgiveness is a process. When we grapple with unforgiveness, there's usually a moment when conviction strikes and we have to acknowledge our part and get right with God. Then we can move toward the other person, humbly acknowledge any wrongdoing on our part, and release the person of the debt they caused in the relationship. Otherwise, we end up holding on to unforgiveness and it only hurts us. When we don't do anything about the fox, he destroys the relationships we care so much about. But if we catch unforgiveness and properly displace it fast enough, we have the opportunity to fix or save what's left.

# Discussion Questions

1. Have you been in a situation where you just could not forgive someone? How did it affect you?

2. This week's scripture says that if we don't forgive others, God will not forgive us. What do you think that means? What does that tell us about the value God places on forgiveness?

3. Is there someone you are currently struggling to forgive? What steps can you take to help yourself get right with God?

4. Think of a time when someone forgave you. What happened, and how did you feel afterward? Share with your family.

## Family Activity

Read through the story of Joseph in Genesis 42–50 and act out the story of Joseph forgiving his brothers. Get creative with costumes. You can even make a set or draw a background (younger kids may love doing this). Allow the story to be an example of how powerful it is to forgive, even when you don't feel like it.

## Action of the Week

Pray each day for God to reveal to you any unforgiveness you are harboring toward people in your life. When God brings someone to mind, go to them and ask for forgiveness. If that's not workable, say to yourself, "I choose to forgive this person," and ask God to change your heart. When situations happen within your family this week, be merciful.

## Guided Prayer

Dear God, thank You for the immense mercy You have shown us. We pray for any unforgiveness we're holding on to and ask You to help us release it this week. Thank You for the strength You give us to forgive even when it is difficult, and help us remember that You are with us every step of the way. In Jesus's name, Amen.

# Looking the Part or Exemplifying It?

*Be careful not to practice your righteousness in front of others to be seen by them. If you do, you will have no reward from your Father in Heaven.*

—MATTHEW 6:1

**Have you ever watched** golf on TV? Professional golfers certainly look the part. They have perfectly pressed pants paired with collared shirts, crisp-white golf shoes, and hats—all from the same athletic brand because they have most likely been sponsored by the company.

It reminds us of the difference between the Pharisees and the disciples. You see, the disciples didn't look religious. Remember, they left everything to follow Jesus. We never read in the Bible about how impressive their overcoats or fishing boats were. Their goodness came through in their actions.

On the other hand, the Pharisees preached but didn't practice what they preached. They intended all their deeds to be seen by others. Instead of tithing out of sacrifice from the produce they had, they tithed spices so that people saw them giving—but it wasn't out of a sacrificial heart. Furthermore, they refused to show others mercy, justice, or faithfulness. And Jesus rebuked their behavior. He didn't want followers who took more pride in how things looked on the outside than what was in their own hearts.

Pride has always been a deceptive tool of the enemy. The world will tell you that how things look is what's important. Although a beautiful house and fancy cars and nice clothes are not necessarily bad, they can become detrimental to our focus if we give them more attention than our heart and its attitudes. God wants our hearts to be focused on Him and the needs of others, and when we serve others with humility in our hearts, He pours blessing upon us. The disciples didn't have much, but they were always taken care of and could attest to God's blessing on their lives.

# Discussion Questions

1. What are some examples of pride that you can think of?

2. Who is someone you know who serves others with humility? How has their example impacted you?

3. Have you ever seen someone who has acted out of pride? How have you struggled with it?

4. Can you think of a time when you did something good just to be seen doing it? How did you feel about it afterward?

## Family Activity

Cast appearances aside! Go out to run an errand wearing something silly that you might normally be embarrassed to wear in public. If your family has young kids, let the kids dress the parents any way they want, without the parents being able to veto it. Afterward, discuss how this made you feel. Did people give you any looks or make any comments that made you feel lesser than?

## Action of the Week

Memorize Matthew 23:12, which says, "For those who exalt themselves will be humbled, and those who humble themselves will be exalted." Discuss as a family how pride and humility are different, and talk about ways your family can live a humble life that honors God.

## Guided Prayer

Lord, root out any pride in our hearts that lets us believe we can do this life without You. Help us model You with humility and have hearts to serve others like You did. In Jesus's name, Amen.

# Don't Dunk on Them

*Whoever derides their neighbor has no sense,*
*but the one who has understanding holds*
*their tongue.*

—PROVERBS 11:12–13

**A few years ago,** our younger two boys built a box fort on our patio. We momentarily felt so proud they weren't just trying to spend more time on screens all day that we agreed to their request to sleep in it. Our little backyard was totally enclosed, and we often got critters running across a fence that backed up to a large warehouse behind our house.

About thirty minutes after they laid down outside, our nine-year-old thought he heard a parent walking near him, but opened his eyes to see a giant opossum wandering along the fence. He ran inside, freaking out, leaving the seven-year-old all alone, sleeping in the backyard. When our seven-year-old calmly wandered in the next morning and discovered his big brother had run from the opossum, he immediately said, "Of course, he's a huge wimp," and with an enormous smile, reserved for the extremely occasional moments when little brothers win, he strutted upstairs for a little more shut-eye.

What is that thing? The thing in our hearts that immediately pivots from personal success to pushing others down. He had every right to be proud of himself for sleeping outside all night, but why did his heart see it as an opportunity to shove his brother down?

There is a natural desire to lift ourselves up by pushing others down. This week's verse makes clear that this impulse doesn't help; it actually hurts us. Every time we "dunk" on someone in our family or circle of friends, we are setting ourselves up to receive the same treatment down the line. When you compete against yourself and stop focusing on others' flaws or victories, you'll see peace grow in your family.

# Discussion Questions

1. Why do our victories make us want to push others down?

2. Can you think of a time someone was ungracious in victory toward you? How did it make you feel?

3. How did Jesus treat others? How does His example influence how we treat those we perceive ourselves to be better than?

4. The Bible says, "The one who has understanding holds their tongue." What do you think this tells us about how to respond when we feel like "dunking" on someone else?

## Family Activity

Go around the table and have each person describe an amazing victory in their life, whether in sports, work, or some other area. Try to tell the story without speaking negatively of anyone else, especially if, as in a race or a contest, your victory meant someone else's direct loss. Notice how aggressively we tend to tell our victory stories (if we do) by being critical of the person who loses.

## Action of the Week

For an entire week, try not to belittle anyone else, even in jest. As this week's verse directs us, refuse to speak negatively of anyone—for any reason—for a whole week.

## Guided Prayer

Dear Lord, help us be gracious in victory and defeat. Help us use kindness to bind our family together. Thank You, Jesus. Amen.

# The Gift from God

*For it is by grace you have been saved, through faith—and this is not from yourselves, it is the gift of God—not by works, so that no one can boast.*

—EPHESIANS 2:8–9

**When Kristen was in junior high,** she entered a drawing for a free, brand-new Ford Mustang convertible. Even though she didn't have her driver's license, she imagined winning a free car would be pretty cool. A few weeks later, the company called to say she had won the Mustang, but she had to come to a meeting where she was part of another group of finalists for the drawing. It took about ten minutes to realize that there was nothing *free* about the Mustang convertible.

It can be so hard to believe that the grace that God has given to us is free. Most things we run into in life have fine print, loopholes, and conditions. But God's grace is absolutely free and unconditional. More important, it is only possible through Him, and because we have received it, we have a responsibility to share it with others. If it was something we had to earn, we might end up with measuring sticks like the Pharisees, trying to make sure everyone else lines up with our standards.

Jesus saw our deep need for grace—the unmerited, unearned love and favor of God—and extended it through the cross. What sets Christianity apart from all other religions is that God sent His Son to pay the price for all of us.

Jesus tells us to come to Him just as we are. His grace was costly, but He gives it out freely to anyone who acknowledges that they are a sinner in need of a Savior.

# Discussion Questions

1. How does it feel to know that God's grace is absolutely free? Have you ever felt you had to earn it? What else in life, if anything, do we get for free?

2. Can you describe a time in your life when you experienced grace? How did that make you feel?

3. Who is the most difficult person in your life to extend grace to and why?

4. Is it more difficult for you to extend grace to others or to yourself? Why do you think that is?

## Family Activity

As an experiment, get two balloons. Fill one with air and fill the other with air and a bit of water. You will also need a candle and a lighter. Have an adult put the air-filled balloon near the fire. It will inevitably burst, like many of us do in heated and difficult situations. Now put the balloon filled with air and water near the flame. You'll see that the fire will leave a mark, but with the water inside, the balloon won't burst—just as we can withstand difficult situations when we're filled with the Holy Spirit. This is God's grace in our lives.

## Action of the Week

As a family, extend grace to one another this week. In the inevitable moments when someone treats you unkindly or unfairly, instead of making those moments a crisis, use them to extend grace like the grace God has given to you— even if the other person hasn't apologized for the hurt, or you feel they haven't earned your forgiveness.

## Guided Prayer

Thank You, God, for the gift of grace that You gave us through Jesus's death on the cross. Help us accept that truth in our own lives and extend it to others when given the opportunity. May Your grace be manifested in the life of our family this week. In Jesus's name, Amen.

# Controlling Our Impulses

*It teaches us to say "No" to ungodliness and worldly passions, and to live self-controlled, upright and godly lives in this present age.*

—TITUS 2:12

**When you have had** a terrible day, it's difficult not to explode in frustration. Often our attitude sets the tone for what we can accomplish. In the book of Nehemiah, we meet a man with a big task. The Lord puts on Nehemiah's heart that he is to rebuild the walls around the city, which has been destroyed. From the beginning, he faces opposition and discouragement. For any progress he makes, he also runs into setbacks.

Nehemiah is frustrated, but he chooses to trust God rather than lashing out in anger. Giving in to anger would be a lot easier than exhibiting self-control, but the problem with that course of action is it never solves the issue of the anger. Self-control is choosing to trust God in the midst of difficulty without giving in to our emotional impulses.

God made each of us with different weaknesses. Some of us start eating donuts and can't stop. Others hate donuts but might lash out in anger if someone says something harsh. Still others might not give in to anger, but they may spend more money than they have in the bank. If we give in to these temptations, we might end up unhealthy, in a conflict, or broke! We also limit our opportunities to represent God well. If we trust that God rewards our self-control, we allow Him to work in our lives, bringing us health and good relationships, and providing enough to meet our needs.

# Discussion Questions

1. What area of self-control is most difficult for you? Some examples might be things like anger, words, food, or money.

2. Can you think of a time when you gave in to anger and regretted it? How can you handle it differently the next time?

3. Was there ever a time in your life when you demonstrated self-control and God blessed your choice? What happened? Share with your family.

4. What setbacks like Nehemiah's have you run into when trying to do something you thought was a good thing? How did it turn out?

## *Family Activity*

Play Jenga as a family. This game is tricky! One careless move can cause the whole tower to come tumbling down. Use the game as an opportunity to remember that when you're not careful, the consequences can be swift and bigger than you anticipated. If there's time, play more than once. Proceed more carefully the second time and practice handling your frustration in healthy ways when things don't go the way you hope.

## Action of the Week

Each night at dinner, read a verse from Proverbs about self-control. Apply the wisdom from each verse to your life and reflect on how self-control can make or break you growing into what God wants for you.
(Proverbs 14:17, 15:1, 18, 17:27, 25:27–28)

## Guided Prayer

Dear God, help us continuously grow in self-control as we become more like You. When our circumstances are disappointing or discouraging, help us not give in to temptation but instead trust You in all things. In Jesus's name, Amen.

# Trying Does Count

*But the Lord said to my father David, "You did well to have it in your heart to build a temple for my Name."*

—2 CHRONICLES 6:8

**Our son Graham is** the third boy in the family. With two older brothers, he is always trying to measure up and stand out. One year, for Kristen's birthday, he picked some wildflowers from a field he saw on his route walking to school and put them in a vase with water under his bed. On the vase, he taped a card that read, "Graham picked these flowers for mom."

Unfortunately, there wasn't much water in the vase, and it eventually spilled, leaving the flowers shriveled and dead. And because Graham had wanted it to be a secret, none of us knew. In the meantime, Luke took the boys to the store the night before Kristen's birthday to pick out a huge bouquet of flowers. The next morning, we heard commotion and found Graham's empty vase next to the other vase of giant, beautiful flowers. Graham cried and cried, believing he had ruined Kristen's birthday, that she'd be upset because he had given her an empty vase.

Well, Kristen told him her favorite part of her birthday was that he thought ahead without being reminded, and that he had wanted to bless her with something on her birthday. It didn't matter that the plan hadn't exactly worked out; what mattered was the heart behind it.

David finds himself in a similar situation, when after a life on the battlefields he wants to build a grand temple in which to worship. He wants to be the leader that moves people from the temporary to the permanent. God denies David's request but, in the verse on page 145, gives him credit for his heart's desire. Even though David won't be able to do it, God is blessed by his heart toward it.

Have you had a similar goal in your family? Something you wanted to make happen, but for whatever reason your efforts did not produce the outcome you hoped for? Take comfort today in the God who doesn't need our outcomes but wants our hearts, who delights in our desires even when they don't quite make it to fruition.

# Discussion Questions

1. Why do you think David wanted to build God a temple?

2. Have you ever tried to do something important to you that didn't really work out? What happened?

3. Why is it kind to bless people for intentions as well as accomplishments?

4. What is one of the nicest things someone has tried to do for you? Why?

## Family Activity

Get out a set of blocks or Legos (or even a deck of playing cards). Build the highest tower possible, block by block, until it falls over. Rather than groaning when the tower falls, cheer at how well you did and how high you were able to get the tower. The point is to emphasize trying your best and accepting the results.

## Action of the Week

Try to notice the intentions or efforts of others. Say things like "Thank you for working so hard" or "I see your effort." Whether someone is playing a sport, doing an art project, or emptying the dishwasher, for this week, focus your words on acknowledging people for their efforts.

## Guided Prayer

Dear Lord, help us focus on the intentions of those who love us. We want to see our loved ones in the kindest possible light. Thank You, Jesus. Amen.

# Choose God, Not Certainty

---

*Or those eighteen who died when the tower in Siloam fell on them—do you think they were more guilty than all the others living in Jerusalem? I tell you, no! But unless you repent, you too will all perish.*

—LUKE 13:4-5

---

**Do you ever see someone** you know hurting and feel they are to blame for it?

Because we're human, we tend to judge others. We do this by processing their external struggles or successes as earned outcomes of their choices, whether good or bad. We see people doing good as "good" and people doing bad as "bad."

We tend to see short-term blessings or struggles as evidence of God's pleasure or disappointment with us. A careful reading of scripture, however, requires us to see that God's bigger plans, which sometimes take generations to unfold, can't always be understood by us in the present moment. But God sees it all.

This is what Jesus is getting at in this week's verse. When questioned about why a certain natural disaster has happened, Jesus points out that the people involved aren't being punished for bad deeds. Matthew 5:45 says that rain falls on both the righteous and the unrighteous. The only certainty is our need to get right with God. Every situation, whether good or bad, every outcome, whether fair or unfair, has an intended purpose of drawing you closer through repentance to God.

We must protect our families from strong judgments of others, especially when only God knows the whole story. If a grade is not good, that doesn't have to mean the test taker is lazy. If a doctor brings a bad prognosis, it isn't necessarily because the patient made bad choices. God is in charge. For our part, we must live in love, comfort those around us, and make sure we are right with God when the rain comes.

# Discussion Questions

1. Do you always assume you know why certain things happen to others? Why or why not?

2. Have you ever had something bad come your way and wonder if God was punishing you?

3. Why is this topic a key to helping people in pain? What do you think God wants us to get out of these verses?

4. Is it sometimes hard to understand when good things happen to people who don't seem to deserve them? How do you think Jesus would tell us to look at these situations?

## Family Activity

Play the "I Don't Know" game. Each person at the table should try to think of three or four questions that are seemingly impossible to answer, like "How many windows are there in New York City?" or "Which state has the most worms in it?" Go around writing down your guesses and try to think of good reasons for your answers. You can even do a little research to see if you can find the answers, but accept that you may not be able to track them down. Bonus points for the person who asks the most impossible question!

## Action of the Week

Practice a no-judgment mantra: Train yourself not to make judgments for a week. When you hear of some new celebrity scandal or news story, or even a bit of gossip at school or work, say out loud, "I have no idea why that happened." Even if you feel like you probably know some of the issues involved, don't try to guess, just say the mantra.

## Guided Prayer

God, thank You for being in control of why things happen. Help us always give others the benefit of the doubt. Help us replace judgment with kindness. In Jesus's name, Amen.

# God Wants to Use Broken Pieces

*Through the offspring the Lord gives you by this young woman, may your family be like that of Perez, whom Tamar bore to Judah.*

—RUTH 4:12

**Every winter, our family** does a big puzzle. We tinker away on a beautiful landscape with 1,000 pieces in it, slowly letting it take shape. Inevitably, when there a few dozen pieces left, one of us pockets one to try and be the person who gets the moment of completion by sliding in the last piece. A little sneaky, yes, but understandable, too.

God doesn't hide our broken pieces; He uses them. The stuff in our life that does not fit or that causes us shame is what He loves to leverage for His glory. God uses the pieces that do not fit as part of His plan for redemption.

We can't help but be struck by the beauty and humor in the way the Bible presents things in comparison to the way we view them. In Ruth 4, the elders of the community are blessing Ruth and Boaz on their upcoming marriage, and they reference the story of Tamar from Genesis 38.

Tamar's story has death, divorce, abuse, family infighting, and tragedy. Yet, because she perseveres and has a son, the Bible sees her as a blessed heroine. To Ruth, who has dealt with her own family pain, Tamar is almost aspirational. It's a crazy story from Genesis, but to summarize, God allows Tamar to have a son in the family line that also produces David and Jesus Christ. This isn't to say that we can only become heroes by having sons or following any other specific path. The point is that even though Tamar suffers through some seriously complicated stuff, she is still used by God in a wonderful way.

You may wish that your family had a different story. There may be broken pieces or mistakes that are sometimes a bit embarrassing or confusing for you to navigate. That's okay. But you must also know that God does not look at your family like a bunch of broken pieces. He sees great potential for good in all of us.

# Discussion Questions

1. Do you think your family is a "normal" family? Why or why not?

2. Where does the pressure we feel to be normal come from?

3. Have you ever seen God use something you were ashamed of or embarrassed about in a good way?

4. What do you think makes someone a hero? What does it mean to be a hero for God as opposed to being a hero in the world's eyes?

## Family Activity

Make a puzzle and then try to solve it. Get thick card stock and draw pieces on it. You can model it after a puzzle you have seen before or just draw funny shapes. Then cut it out with scissors and try to put the puzzle together. It won't completely work—the pieces won't fit in the same way that a professionally produced puzzle fits together—but that's the fun!

## Action of the Week

In conversation with others, try to notice every time you minimize things you are embarrassed about or embellish things you are proud of. Observe how often you are tempted to change your story to fit the conversation you are in. Share the occurrences with your family.

## Guided Prayer

God, help us see the broken parts of our family as part of Your plan and not something to be embarrassed about. Help us trust You to use it all for good. In Jesus's name, Amen.

# Everyone Likes Good News

---

*And he kissed all his brothers and wept*
*over them. Afterward his brothers talked*
*with him. When the news reached Pharaoh's*
*palace that Joseph's brothers had come,*
*Pharaoh and all his officials were pleased.*

—GENESIS 45:15–16

---

**Does anyone in your family** watch those predictable Hallmark holiday movies? The ones where the big-city heroine falls in love in a small town, usually over a tree-decorating party or a cookie-baking competition? It doesn't matter if the movies have similar plotlines, they underpin something very important for families: They feel good to watch, and people love positive news.

In our verse for this week, why is Pharaoh happy when he hears the news of Joseph's brothers arriving? Because Pharaoh undoubtedly knows Joseph's painful origin story after all these years, he understands how powerful a positive reconnection for Joseph will be. Even people who don't know God love seeing broken things put back together. If that's true, how much more focused on the good should God's people be?

Every restored relationship is a miracle. Every family still making it and loving one another is to be praised. Every marriage still trying is to be commended. Every child reading the Bible is to be encouraged. If we have Jesus, we must have eyes to see good all around.

The power of positive thinking can be easily twisted in many cases. When we believe positive thinking guarantees that good things will happen, we have misread the Bible. The proper reaction is not to abandon positive thinking, it's to properly channel it. Choosing to see the good in the world around us doesn't force God to bless us, but it does make us happier.

Optimism is braver than cynicism and joy has more impact than negativity. Trying again with someone has more power than writing them off. When we lean out and try to share good news, it makes an impact. When you choose to see the good in your family, blessing them for as many positive things as you can see in them, you are loving well.

# Discussion Questions

1. Do you ever struggle to see the good in things or people? Do you sometimes find it scary to think positively?

2. Why do you think bad news travels faster than good news?

3. Who is the most positive person in your family?

4. Can you think of any other restored relationships in the Bible? What are the similarities between those stories and Joseph's story?

## Family Activity

Make a family newspaper called *The "Good News" News*. Create a front page with headlines and short articles that highlight good things your family is involved in. To really get into it, draw some pictures and interview one another. The point is to highlight and celebrate the positive things happening in your family.

## Action of the Week

This week, start every interaction with your close family members with the exclamation, "Good news . . ." See how your interactions change when you force yourself to focus on the present and the positive. Even if you need to discuss a problem, try to start on a positive note.

## Guided Prayer

God, thank You for bringing the good news through Jesus. Help us bring good news to others and focus on the good. In Jesus's name, Amen.

# A Final Word

**You made it!** Fifty-two weeks of diving into God's Word together as a family, applying it to your life, and seeing God plant seeds in each person in your family. Consider it a large deposit in your family's spiritual bank account.

When we moved to California, we lived in a home with a brick patio with planters surrounding it. We filled it with bougainvillea, as well as a mini lime tree and an assortment of other flowers that filled the backyard with beauty. Some grew like crazy while others barely made it. With any investment, you don't know how or when you will see the return made. But God's Word promises to never return void. Just like we had to tend to these plants with food, water, and trimming, we encourage you to continue to nurture your family's spiritual walk with another devotional or by working through a book of the Bible like Proverbs.

God will use the closeness that was cultivated through the time shared with His Word. Continue to use the tools that your family found fun and helpful from the activities and actions and you'll be amazed at what God does!

# ACKNOWLEDGMENTS

We are so grateful for the opportunity to encourage your family with God's Word. This book wouldn't exist if our parents hadn't cultivated a love for God's Word in us from an early age. We are incredibly grateful for the support our siblings and our local church, Good News in the Neighborhood, have made in our lives. We love our weekly newsletter readers who give us a voice into their lives every Saturday morning with what God is teaching us. Lastly, we want to thank Rockridge Press for this opportunity and all the hands who helped birth this book into existence.

# ABOUT THE AUTHORS

 We are **Luke** and **Kristen MacDonald**, high school sweethearts doing our best to love and live for Jesus in this crazy world. Luke attended Moody Bible Institute and Talbot Seminary, receiving a BA in biblical studies and an MA in biblical exposition. Kristen studied early childhood education at Cedarville and Judson Universities. Together we lead Good News in the Neighborhood, a multiethnic, Bible-teaching, life-giving church in the northwest suburbs of Chicago. Our family is full and fun. We have four kids: Carter, Reid, Graham, and Felicity. Between sports and lively personalities, you will rarely find a dull moment at our house! If you want to sign up for our newsletter "Good News Weekly," which drops every Saturday morning, visit GoodNewsInTheNeighborhood .substack.com.